Guitar Chord Songbook

The following songs are the property of:

Bourne Co.
Music Publishers
5 West 37th Street
New York, NY 10018

BABY MINE
I'M WISHING

Disney characters and artwork © Disney Enterprises, Inc.

ISBN 978-1-4234-7007-6

7777 W. BLUEMOUND RD. P.O. BOX 13819 MILWAUKEE, WI 53213

For all works contained herein:
Unauthorized copying, arranging, adapting, recording, Internet posting, public performance,
or other distribution of the printed music in this publication is an infringement of copyright.
Infringers are liable under the law.

Visit Hal Leonard Online at
www.halleonard.com

Guitar Chord Songbook

Contents

Alice in Wonderland

from Walt Disney's ALICE IN WONDERLAND

Words by Bob Hilliard
Music by Sammy Fain

Melody:

Al - ice   in   Won-der-land.

G°7   G   D7   Am7   F#7   Bm7   E7   A7

Verse 1

G°7 G D7 G
Al - ice in   Wonderland.

Am7   D7   G
How do you get to Wonderland?

Am7   D7   G
Over the hill or underland

   Am7   D7   G
Or just be - hind the tree?

Verse 2

G°7 G   D7 G
When clouds go   rolling by,

Am7   D7   G
They roll a - way and leave the sky.

Am7   D7   G
Where is the land be - yond the eye

   F#7   Bm7 E7
That people cannot see?

© 1951 Walt Disney Music Company
Copyright Renewed
All Rights Reserved   Used by Permission

Bridge

Am7   D7   G
Where can it be?

Am7   D7   G
Where do   stars go?

Am7   D7   G
Where is the crescent moon?

F♯7   Bm7   E7
They must be some - where

Am7   D7
In the sunny after - noon.

Verse 3

G°7 G D7   G
Al - ice in   Wonderland.

Am7   D7   G
Where is the path to Wonderland?

Am7   D7   G   A7
Over the hill or here or there?

Am7 D7   G
I won - der   where.

Baby Mine

from Walt Disney's DUMBO

Words by Ned Washington
Music by Frank Churchill

Melody:

Ba - by   mine ___ don't you

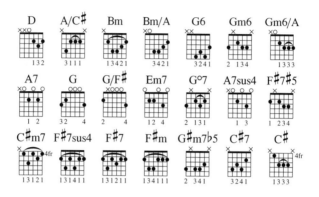

Verse 1

D   A/C# Bm Bm/A   G6 Gm6 Gm6/A A7
Ba - by   mine ___ don't you cry.

D   A/C# Bm Bm/A   G6 Gm6 Gm6/A A7
Ba - by   mine ___ dry your eye.

G   G/F# Em7   G6
Rest your ____ head close to my heart,

    G°7   D Em7 D A7sus4
Never to part, baby of mine.

Copyright © 1941 by Walt Disney Productions
Copyright Renewed
World Rights Controlled by Bourne Co. (ASCAP)
International Copyright Secured   All Rights Reserved

Verse 2

D A/C♯ Bm Bm/A   G6 Gm6 Gm6/A A7
Lit - tle   one ____ when you play,

D   A/C♯ Bm Bm/A   G6 Gm6 Gm6/A A7
Don't you   mind ___ what they say.

G G/F♯ Em7   G6
Let those eyes sparkle and shine,

      G°7   D Em7 D F♯7♯5
Never a tear, baby of mine.

Bridge

Bm   C♯m7 F♯7sus4 F♯7
If they knew sweet little you,

Bm   C♯m7 F♯7sus4 F♯7
They'd end up loving you too.

Bm   F♯m
All those same people who scold you,

Bm   G♯m7♭5 C♯7   F♯m C♯ Em7 A7
What they'd give   just for the right to hold you.

Verse 3

D   A/C♯ Bm Bm/A   G6 Gm6 Gm6/A A7
From your   head ____ to your toes,

D   A/C♯ Bm Bm/A   G6 Gm6 Gm6/A A7
You're not   much, ___ goodness knows,

G G/F♯ Em7   G6
But you're so precious to me,

      G°7   D
Cute as can be, baby of mine.

The Ballad of Davy Crockett

from Walt Disney's DAVY CROCKETT

Words by Tom Blackburn
Music by George Bruns

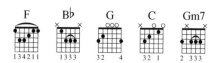

Verse 1

F	B♭ F

Born on a mountaintop in Tennes - see,

                  G   **C**
Greenest state in the land of the free.

F   **B♭**   **Gm7**
Raised in the woods so's he knew ev'ry tree,

C   **F**
Kilt him a b'ar when he was only three.

Chorus 1

F **B♭** **F**
Davy, Davy Crockett,

C   **F**
King of the wild fron - tier!

Verse 2

     F   **B♭**   **F**
In eighteen thirteen the Creeks up - rose,

                 G   **C**
Addin' redskin arrows to the country's woes.

     F   **B♭**   **Gm7**
Now Injun fightin' is somethin' he knows,

     C   **F**
So he shoulders his rifle an' off he goes.

Chorus 2

F **B♭** **F**
Davy, Davy Crockett,

  C   **F**
The man who don't know fear!

© 1954 Wonderland Music Company, Inc.
Copyright Renewed
All Rights Reserved   Used by Permission

The Bare Necessities
from Walt Disney's THE JUNGLE BOOK

Words and Music by
Terry Gilkyson

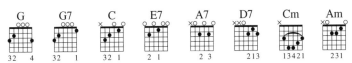

Verse

    N.C.   **G**   **G7**
Look for the   bare ne-cessities,

    C
The simple bare necessities,

    G7   **E7**   **A7**
For-get about your worries and your strife.

D7   **G**   **G7**
    I mean the   bare ne-cessities

    C
Or Mother Nature's recipes

    G   **E7**   **A7**   **D7** **G**
That bring the bare ne-cessities___ of life.

        D7   **G**
Wherever I wander, wherever I roam,

        D7   **G**
I couldn't be fonder of my big home.

G7   **C**   **Cm**
    The bees are buzzin' in the tree

        G   **A7**
To make some honey just for me,

    Am   **C**   **D7**   **G**
The bare ne-cessities of life will come to you.

© 1964 Wonderland Music Company, Inc.
Copyright Renewed
All Rights Reserved   Used by Permission

Be Our Guest

from Walt Disney's BEAUTY AND THE BEAST

Lyrics by Howard Ashman
Music by Alan Menken

Melody:

Be   our   guest!   Be   our

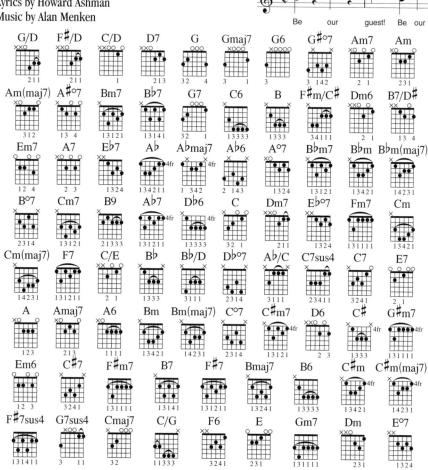

Intro   Spoken: Lumiere: *Ma chere Mademoiselle,*

G/D

F♯/D
It is with deepest pride and greatest pleasure

C/D
That we welcome you tonight.

And now, we invite you to relax.
D7
Let us pull up a chair as dining room proudly presents your dinner!

© 1991 Walt Disney Music Company and Wonderland Music Company, Inc.
All Rights Reserved   Used by Permission

Verse 1

       G   **Gmaj7**
Be our guest! Be our guest!

G6   **G**
Put our service to the test.

                  G$\sharp$°7
Tie your napkin 'round your neck, *cherie*,

Am7   **D7**
And we'll provide the rest.

         Am   **Am(maj7)**
Soup du - jour! Hot hors d'oeuvres!

     Am7   **D7**
Why, we only live to serve.

     Am7   **A$\sharp$°7**
Try the grey stuff. It's de - licious!

     Bm7   **B$\flat$7**   **Am7**
Don't be - lieve me? Ask the dishes!

D7   **G**   **Gmaj7**
They can sing! They can dance!

       G6
After all, Miss, this is France!

G   **G7**   **C6**
   And a dinner here is never second best.

N.C.   **B**   **F$\sharp$m/C$\sharp$** **Dm6**
Go on, un - fold your ___ men - u.

B7/D$\sharp$ **Em7**   **A7**   **Am7**
Take a glance and then ___ you'll be our guest,

      D7   **G**   **E$\flat$7**
Oui, our guest. Be our guest!

Verse 2

       Ab   Abmaj7
Beef ra - gout! Cheese souf - flé!

     Ab6   Ab
Pie and pudding *"en flam - bé!"*

                A°7   Bbm7   Eb7
We'll prepare and serve with flair a culi - nary caba - ret.

     Bbm   Bbm(maj7)
You're a - lone and you're scared,

     Bbm7   Eb7
But the banquets all pre - pared.

     Bbm7   B°7
No one's gloomy or com - plaining

     Cm7   B9   Bbm7
While the flatware's enter - taining.

Eb7 Ab   Abmaj7   Ab6   Ab
We tell jokes. I do tricks with my fellow candle - sticks.

          Abmaj7 Ab7   Db6
Mugs: And it's all in perfect   taste. That you can bet!

   N.C.   C   Dm7   Eb°7
All: Come on and lift your ____ glass.

   Fm7   Bb7   Bbm7
You've won your own free pass ____ to be our guest.

         Eb7   Cm   Cm(maj7) F7
Lumiere: If you're stressed it's fine dining we sug - gest.

     Bbm7   Fm7 Eb7 Ab   C
All: Be our guest! Be our guest! Be our guest!

Bridge

     Fm7   C/E
Lumiere: Life is so unnerving for a servant who's not serving.

   E♭°7   A♭7   B♭ B♭/D
He's not whole without a soul to wait up - on.

D♭°7   A♭/C Fm7
Ah, those good old days when we were useful.

B♭m7   C7sus4 C7
Suddenly, those good old days are gone.

   Fm7   C/E
Ten years we've been rusting, needing so much more than dusting.

   E♭°7   B♭/D
Needing exercise, a chance to use our skills.

D♭°7   A♭ Fm7
Most days we just lay around the castle.

B♭m7   E♭7
Flabby fat and lazy. You walked in, *and oopsadaisy!*

Verse 3

E7 A   Amaj7
It's a guest! It's a guest!

        A6   A
Sakes a - live, well, I'll be blessed.

                      $A^{\sharp\circ}7$
Wine's been poured, and thank the Lord,

      Bm7   E7
I've had the napkins freshly pressed.

      Bm   Bm(maj7)
With des - sert she'll want tea.

      Bm7   E7
And, my dear, that's fine with me.

      Bm7 $C^{\circ}7$
While the cups do their soft-shoeing

  $C^{\sharp}m7$ C7 Bm7
I'll be bubbling! I'll be brewing!

E7 A   Amaj7
I'll get warm, piping hot.

     A6   A
Heaven sakes! Is that a spot? Clean it up…

  Amaj7 A7   D6
We want the company im - pressed!

N.C. $C^{\sharp}$ $G^{\sharp}m7$
We've got a lot _____ to do.

Em6 $C^{\sharp}7$ $F^{\sharp}m7$ B7   Bm
  Is it one lump or two ___ for you, our guest?

       E7 $C^{\sharp}m7$ $F^{\sharp}7$
All: She's our guest! Mrs. Potts: She's our guest! She's our guest!

Verse 4

B   **Bmaj7**   **B6**   **B**
Be our guest! Be our guest! Our com - mand is your re - quest.

       C°7   **C♯m**   **F♯7**
It's ten years since we had anybody here, and we're ob - sessed!

C♯m   **C♯m(maj7)** **C♯m7**   **F♯7**
With your meal, with your ease, yes, in - deed, we aim to please.

F♯7sus4   **F♯7**   **G7sus4**
While the candlelight's still glowing, let us help you,

G7   **C**   **Cmaj7**
We'll keep going course by course, one by one!

C6   **C/G**
'Til you shout, *"Enough, I'm done!"*

       Cmaj7 C7   **F6**
Then we'll sing you off to   sleep as you di - gest.

     E   **F♯m7**   **Gm7**
Tonight you'll prop your ___ feet ___ up!

G♯°7 Am7   **D7**
But for now, let's eat ___ up!

Dm   **E°7**   **Dm**
Be our guest! Be our guest! Be our guest!

G7sus4 G7 C
Please, be   our guest!

Beauty and the Beast

from Walt Disney's BEAUTY AND THE BEAST

Lyrics by Howard Ashman
Music by Alan Menken

Melody:

Tale as old as time,

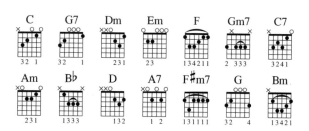

Verse 1

    C   G7 C   Dm
Tale as old as time,   true as it can be.

    C   Em   F   G7
Barely even friends, then somebody bends unexpected - ly.

    C   G7   C   Gm7
Just a little change.   Small, to say the least.

    C7   F   Em   Dm
Both a little scared, neither one pre - pared.

    G7   C   G7 C
Beauty and the Beast.

© 1991 Walt Disney Music Company and Wonderland Music Company, Inc.
All Rights Reserved   Used by Permission

Bridge

    G7   **Em** **F**   **Em**
Ever just the same,   ever a sur - prise.

F   **Em**   **Am**   **B♭** **C**
Ever as be - fore, ever just as sure as the sun will rise.

Verse 2

D   **A7** **D**   **A7**
Tale as old as time,   tune as old as song.

D   **F♯m7**   **G**
Bittersweet and strange, finding you can change,

            A7
Learning you were wrong.

D   **A7** **D**   **Am**
Certain as the sun   rising in the East,

D   **G**   **Em**
Tale as old as time, song as old as rhyme.

A7   **D**
Beauty and the Beast.

Bm   **G**   **Em**
Tale as old as time, song as old as rhyme.

A7   **D**
Beauty and the Beast.

Bella Notte

(This Is the Night)

from Walt Disney's LADY AND THE TRAMP

Words and Music by
Peggy Lee and Sonny Burke

Melody:

This ___ is the night, ___ it's a

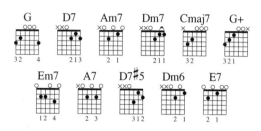

Verse

        G
This is the night, it's a beautiful night,

             D7
And we call it Bella Notte.

          Am7   **D7**
Look at the skies, they have stars in their eyes

        Am7 D7 **G**
On this lovely Bella Notte.

       Dm7
So take the love of your loved one.

         Cmaj7   **G+**   **Cmaj7**
You'll need it a - bout this time

        Em7   **A7**   **Em7**   **A7**
To keep from falling like a star

          Am7   **D7**
When you make that dizzy climb.

D7♯5 **G**   **Dm6**   **E7**
For   this is the night and heavens are right

        Am7 D7 **G**
On this lovely Bella Notte.

© 1952 Walt Disney Music Company
Copyright Renewed
All Rights Reserved   Used by Permission

Bibbidi-Bobbidi-Boo
(The Magic Song)
from Walt Disney's CINDERELLA

Words by Jerry Livingston
Music by Mack David and Al Hoffman

Melody:

Sa - la - ga - doo - la, men-chic - ka boo - la,

F   C7   Bb   Dm   G7

Verse 1

F
Salagadoola, menchicka boola, bibbidi - bobbidi - boo.

C7
Put 'em together and what have you got?

F
Bibbidi - bobbidi - boo.

Verse 2

F
Salagadoola, menchicka boola, bibbidi - bobbidi - boo.

C7
It'll do magic believe it or not,

F
Bibbidi - bobbidi - boo.

Bridge

Bb   F   Dm
Salagadoola means menchicka boole - roo,

G7   C7
But the thingamabob that does the job is bibbidi - bobbidi - boo.

Outro

F
Salagadoola, menchicka boola, bibbidi - bobbidi - boo.

C7
Put 'em together and what have you got?

F
Bibbidi - bobbidi - bibbidi - bobbidi, bibbidi - bobbidi - boo.

© 1948 Walt Disney Music Company
Copyright Renewed
All Rights Reserved   Used by Permission

Best of Friends

from Walt Disney's
THE FOX AND THE HOUND

Words by Stan Fidel
Music by Richard Johnston

Melody:

When you're the best of friends _____

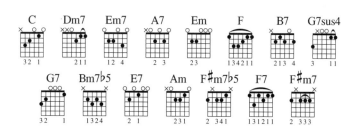

C	Dm7	Em7	A7	Em	F	B7	G7sus4

G7	Bm7♭5	E7	Am	F#m7♭5	F7	F#m7

Verse 1

               C   **Dm7**
When you're the best of friends

        C   **Dm7**
Having so much fun togeth - er,

        Em7   **A7**
You're not even aware you're such a funny pair.

Dm7   **Em**   **F**   **B7**   **G7sus4**
You're the ___ best ___ of ___ friends.

Verse 2

   G7   **C**   **Dm7**
Life's a happy game,

         C   **Dm7**
You could clown around for - ever.

    Em7   **A7**
Neither of you sees your nat'ral boundaries.

Dm7   **Em**   **F** **G7** **C**
Life's one ___ hap - py ___ game.

© 1977 Walt Disney Music Company and Wonderland Music Company, Inc.
Copyright Renewed
All Rights Reserved   Used by Permission

Bridge

<pre>
Dm7   G7   Dm7   G7
If only the world wouldn't get in the way,

Em7   A7   Em7   A7
If only people would just let you play.

Dm7   Em7   F
They'll say you're both being fools,

Bm7b5   E7   Am
You're breaking all the rules.

F#m7b5   F7   Dm7
They can't understand ___ your magic wonderland.
</pre>

Outro

<pre>
G7   C   Dm7
When you're the best of friends,

        C   Dm7
Sharing all that you discov - er,

        Em7
When these moments have passed

        A7
Will that friendship last?

F#m7   B7
Who can say if there's a way?

Em7   A7   Dm7
How I hope,   I hope it's never ends,

        G7sus4   G7 C   Dm7 C
'Cause you're the best of   friends.
</pre>

Can You Feel the Love Tonight

from Walt Disney Pictures' THE LION KING

Music by Elton John
Lyrics by Tim Rice

There's a calm _ sur-ren - der

(Capo 1st fret)

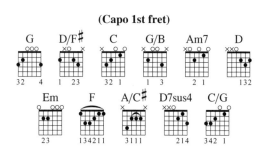

Intro | G   D/F♯ | C   G | C   G/B | D/F♯ G Am7 G/B |

Verse 1
C   G/B   C   G/B
There's a calm surren - der to the rush of day,

C   G/B   Am7   D
When the heat of a rolling wind can be turned away.

C   G/B   C   G/B
An enchanted moment, and it sees me through.

C   Em   F   D
It's enough for this restless warrior just to be with you.

© 1994 Wonderland Music Company, Inc.
All Rights Reserved   Used by Permission

Chorus 1

        G   D/F#   Em   C
And can you feel ___ the love ___ tonight?

G   C   A/C#   D
    It is where __ we ___ are.

C   G/B   Em   C
    It's enough ___ for this wide-eyed wanderer

Am7 G/B C A/C# D
That we got this far.

        G   D/F#   Em   C
And can you feel ___ the love ___ tonight,

G   C   A/C#   D
    How it's laid __ to ___ rest?

C   G/B   Em   C
    It's enough ___ to make kings and vagabonds

  Am7 G/B C D7sus4 C/G   G
Be-lieve the ver - y best.

Interlude   *Repeat Intro*

Verse 2

     C   G/B   C   G/B
There's a time for ev'ryone if they only learn

C   G/B   Am7   D
That the twisting ka-leidoscope moves us all in turn.

C   G/B   C   G/B
There's a rhyme and rea - son to the wild outdoors

C   Em   F   D
When the heart of this star-crossed voyager beats in time with yours.

Chorus 2   *Repeat Chorus 1*

Outro

    C   G/B   Em   C
    It's enough ___ to make kings and vagabonds

  Am7 G/B C D7sus4 C/G   G
Be-lieve the ver-y best.

Candle on the Water
from Walt Disney's PETE'S DRAGON

Words and Music by Al Kasha
and Joel Hirschhorn

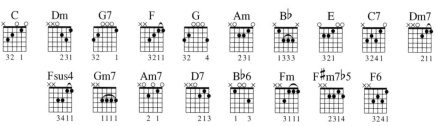

Verse 1	C Dm G7 F G	

Verse 1

     C   Dm G7 F   G
     I'll be your candle on the water,

     C   Am   F   Bb
     My love for you will always burn.

     G E   Am   C7
     I know you're lost and drifting,

     F   C
     But the clouds are lifting,

     F   G7   C   Dm7 G7
     Don't give up; you have somewhere to turn.

Verse 2

     C   Dm G7 F   G
     I'll be your candle on the water,

     C   Am   F   Bb
     'Til ev'ry wave is warm and bright,

     G   E   Am   C7
     My soul is there be-side you,

     F   C
     Let this candle guide you,

     F   G7 C   Dm7 G7
     Soon you'll see a golden stream of light.

© 1976 Walt Disney Music Company and Wonderland Music Company, Inc.
Copyright Renewed
All Rights Reserved   Used by Permission

Bridge

Bb   **C7**   **Fsus4 F**
A cold and friendless tide has found you,

Bb   **C7**   **F   Gm7 F**
Don't let the stormy darkness pull you down.

Am7   **D7**   **G**
I'll paint a ray of hope a-round you,

F   **Em F**   **Bb6**   **G7**
Circling the air, lighted by a prayer.

Verse 3

C   **Dm**   **G7** **F**   **G**
I'll be your candle on the water,

C   **Am** **F**   **Bb**
This flame in-side of me will grow.

G   **E**   **Am**   **C7**
Keep holding on, you'll make it,

F   **C**
Here's my hand, so take it,

F   **G7**   **C7**
Look for me reaching out to show

    F   **Fm** **C** **F#m7b5**
As sure as rivers flow.

F6   **G7**   **C** **G**
I'll never let you go,

F   **G7**   **C** **G**
I'll never let you go,

F   **G7**   **C**   **F C G C**
I'll never let you go.

Chim Chim Cher-ee

from Walt Disney's MARY POPPINS

Words and Music by
Richard M. Sherman and Robert B. Sherman

Melody:

Chim chim-in - ey, chim-chim-in - ey.

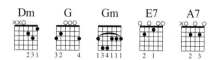

Dm	G	Gm	E7	A7

Chorus 1

Dm   G
Chim chiminey, chim chiminey, chim chim cher - ee!

Gm   Dm   E7   A7
A sweep is as lucky as lucky can be.

Dm   G
Chim chiminey, chim chiminey, chim chim cher - oo!

Gm   Dm   A7   Dm
Good luck will rub off when I shakes 'ands with you.

Gm   Dm   A7   Dm
Or blow me a kiss and that's lucky too.

Verse 1

Dm   G
Now, as the ladder of life 'as been strung,

Gm   Dm   E7   A7
You may think a sweep's on the bottom-most rung.

Verse 2

Dm   G
Though I spend me time in the ashes and smoke,

Gm   Dm   A7 Dm
In this 'ole wide world there's no 'appier bloke.

Chorus 2   *Repeat Chorus 1*

© 1963 Wonderland Music Company, Inc.
Copyright Renewed
All Rights Reserved   Used by Permission

Circle of Life

from Walt Disney Pictures' THE LION KING

Music by Elton John
Lyrics by Tim Rice

Melody:

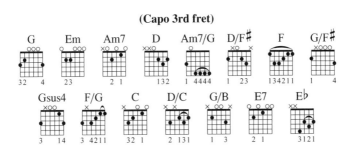

From the day   we ar-rive on the plan - et

(Capo 3rd fret)

G   Em   Am7   D   Am7/G   D/F♯   F   G/F♯

Gsus4   F/G   C   D/C   G/B   E7   E♭

Intro   ‖:G |Em |Am7 |D   :‖

Verse 1

G   Am7/G
From the day we arrive on the plan - et

D/F♯   G
And blinking, step into the sun,

Em   Am7
There's more to be seen than can ever be seen;

F   D
More to do   than can ever be done.

Verse 2

G   Am7/G
Some say eat or be eaten;

D/F♯   G   G/F♯
Some say   live and let live.

Em   Am7
But all are agreed as they join the stampede

F   D
You should never take more than you give.

© 1994 Wonderland Music Company, Inc.
All Rights Reserved   Used by Permission

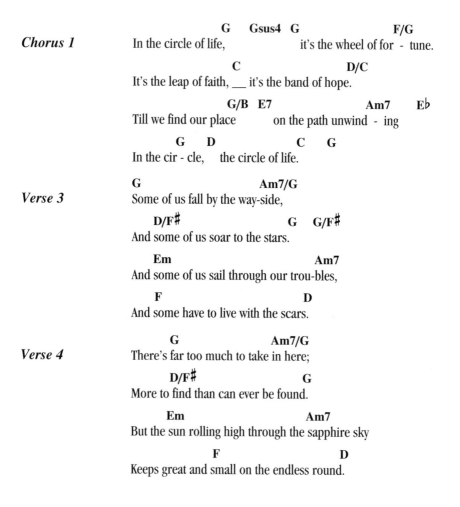

Chorus 1

                      G   Gsus4 G   F/G
In the circle of life,   it's the wheel of for - tune.

                        C   D/C
It's the leap of faith, __ it's the band of hope.

                    G/B E7   Am7   Eb
Till we find our place   on the path unwind - ing

                G   D   C   G
In the cir - cle,   the circle of life.

Verse 3

                G   Am7/G
Some of us fall by the way-side,

                D/F#   G   G/F#
And some of us soar to the stars.

                Em   Am7
And some of us sail through our trou-bles,

                F   D
And some have to live with the scars.

Verse 4

                G   Am7/G
There's far too much to take in here;

                D/F#   G
More to find than can ever be found.

                Em   Am7
But the sun rolling high through the sapphire sky

                  F   D
Keeps great and small on the endless round.

Chorus 2

	G Gsus4 G		F/G

In the circle of life,   it's the wheel of for - tune.

	C		D/C

It's the leap of faith, __ it's the band of hope.

	G/B E7		Am7		Eb

Till we find our place   on the path unwind - ing

	G D		G Gsus4 G

In the cir - cle,   the circle of life.

Outro-Chorus

	F/G		C

It's the wheel of for - tune, yeah, it's the leap of faith.

	D/C		G/B E7

It's the band of hope ____ till we find our place

	Am7		Eb

On the path unwind - ing, yeah,

	G D		C G C G

In the cir - cle,   the circle of life.

E7		Am7 Eb

On the path unwind - ing, yeah,

	G D		C Eb G

In the cir - cle,   the circle of life.

Colors of the Wind

from Walt Disney's POCAHONTAS

Music by Alan Menken
Lyrics by Stephen Schwartz

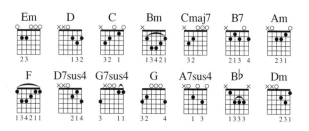

You think I'm an ig-no-rant sav-age,

Em | D | C | Bm | Cmaj7 | B7 | Am

F | D7sus4 | G7sus4 | G | A7sus4 | B♭ | Dm

Intro

    Em   **D**
You think I'm an ignorant savage,

      Em
And you've been so many places,

D
I guess it must be so.

     C   **Bm**   **C**   **Bm**
But still I cannot see, if the savage one is me,

     Em   **Cmaj7**   **B7**
How can there be so much that you don't know?

N.C.   **C**   **Am** **C**
You don't know…

Verse 1

Am   **C**   **Am**
  You think you own whatever land you land on.

C   **Em**
The earth is just a dead thing you can claim.

Am   **F**
But I know ev'ry rock and tree and creature

  D7sus4 **G7sus4**   **Am**
Has a life, has a spirit, has a name.

© 1995 Wonderland Music Company, Inc. and Walt Disney Music Company
All Rights Reserved   Used by Permission

Verse 2

          C   Am
You think the only people who are people

          C   Em
Are the people who look and think like you,

    Am   F
But if you walk in the footsteps of a stranger

        D7sus4   G7sus4   C
You'll learn things you never knew you never knew.

Chorus 1

        Am   Em   F
Have you ever heard the wolf cry to the blue corn moon,

    Am   Em
Or asked the grinning bobcat why he grinned?

      F   G   C
Can you sing with all the voices of the mountain?

Am   F   A7sus4
Can you paint with all the colors of the wind?

    D7sus4   G7sus4   C
Can you paint with all the colors of the wind?

Verse 3

    Am   C   Am
Come run the hidden pine trails of the forest,

    C   Em
Come taste the sun-sweet berries of the earth.

    Am   F
Come roll in all the riches all a - round you,

    D7sus4   G7sus4   Am
And for once never wonder what they're worth.

Verse 4

        C   Am
The rainstorm and the river are my brothers.

        C   Em
The heron and the otter are my friends.

  Am   F
And we are all connected to each other

  D7sus4   G7sus4   C
In a circle, in a hoop that never ends.

Bridge

Em F   C   Am
How high does the sycamore grow?

   B♭   F   G
If you cut it down, then you'll never know.

Chorus 2

F G   Am   Em   G
And you'll never hear the wolf cry to the blue corn moon,

  Am   Em
For whether we are white or copper-skinned,

      F   G   C
We need to sing with all the voices of the mountain,

Am   F   A7sus4
Need to paint with all the colors of the wind.

     Dm   G   Em
You can own the earth and still all you'll own is earth

    F   Am   F   C
Un - til you can paint with all the colors of the wind.

A Dream Is a Wish Your Heart Makes

from Walt Disney's CINDERELLA

Words and Music by Mack David,
Al Hoffman and Jerry Livingston

Melody:

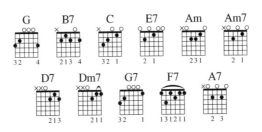

Verse

        G   **B7** **C**
A dream is a wish your heart makes when you're fast a - sleep.

E7 Am   **Am7**
In dreams you will lose your heartaches,

D7   **G**
Whatever you wish for, you keep.

Am7 D7   G
Have faith in your dreams and someday

    Dm7 G7   **C**
Your rainbow will come smiling through.

N.C.   **Am**   **F7**
No matter how your heart is grieving,

    G   **A7**
If you keep on be - lieving,

     Am7   **D7**   **G**
The dream that you wish will come true.

© 1948 Walt Disney Music Company
Copyright Renewed
All Rights Reserved Used by Permission

DISNEY

Friend Like Me

from Walt Disney's ALADDIN

Lyrics by Howard Ashman
Music by Alan Menken

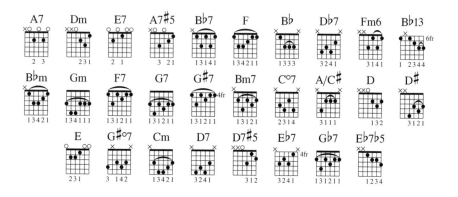

Verse 1

         A7   Dm
Well, Ali Baba had them forty thieves.

       A7   Dm
Schehera - zade had a thousand tales.

        A7   Dm
But, master, you in luck 'cause up your sleeves

       E7   A7#5
You got a brand of magic never fails.

        A7   Dm
You got some power in your corner now,

        A7   Dm
Some heavy ammunition in your camp.

        A7   Dm
You got some punch, pizazz, ya - hoo and how.

        E7
See, all you gotta do is rub that lamp.

A7 N.C.   A7
   And I'll say...

© 1992 Walt Disney Music Company and Wonderland Music Company, Inc.
All Rights Reserved Used by Permission

Chorus 1

Dm   B♭7 A7
Mister A - laddin sir,

    Dm   B♭7
What will your pleasure be?

A7   F   B♭ D♭7
Let me take your order, jot it down.

       F   A7♯5
You ain't never had a friend like me.

Dm B♭7 A7♯5
No, no, no.

Dm   B♭7   A7
Life is your restau - raunt

    Dm   Fm6 B♭13
And I'm your maître d'.

       F   B♭   B♭m
C'- mon whisper what it is ____ you want.

       F   A7
You ain't never had a friend like me.

Dm   B♭7
Yes, sir, we pride ourselves on service.

       Dm   A7   Dm
You're the boss, the king, the shah.

    B♭13
Say what you wish. It's yours!

             Gm   A7
True dish how 'bout a little more baklava?

Dm   B♭7   A7
Have some of column "A".

    Dm   B♭7
Try all of column "B".

A7 F   B♭   D♭7
I'm in the mood to help you, dude,

       F   A7♯5   Dm B♭7 A7
You ain't never had a friend like me.

Interlude

Dm   B♭7 A7
Waahah. Oh my.

Dm   B♭7 A7
Waahah. No, no.

Dm   B♭7   A7 B♭7 A7
Waahah. Nana - na.

Bridge

Dm
Can your friends do this? Can your friends do that?

        F7   **G7 G♯7** **A7 Bm7**
Can your friends pull this out their little ___ hat?

C°7 **A/C♯** **Dm D** **D♯** **E** **F**
Can your friends go poof! *Well, looky___ here.*

     Gm **G♯°7 A7** **Bm7 Cm**
Can your friends go abraca - dabra, let 'er rip

A7   **D7**
And then make the sucker disappear?

Verse 2

      D7   **Gm**
So doncha sit there slack-jawed, buggy-eyed.

     D7   **Gm**
I'm here to answer all your midday prayers.

     D7   **Gm**
You got me bona fide certified.

      A7   **D7♯5**
You got a genie for your chargé d'affaires.

    D7   **Gm**
I got a powerful urge to help you out.

      D7   **Gm**
So whatcha wish I really want to know.

     D7   **Gm**
You got a list that's three miles long ___ no doubt.

      A7   **D7**
Well, all you gotta do is rub like so. And oh.

Outro

Gm   **E♭7** **D7**
Mister A - laddin sir,

   Gm   **E♭7**
Have a wish or two or three.

D7 **B♭**   **B♭7** **E♭7**
I'm on the job, ___ you big nabob.

G♭7 **B♭**
You ain't never had a friend, never had a friend,

   G♭7
You ain't never had a friend, never had a friend,

   E♭7♭5 **D7** **Gm E♭7 D7**
You ain't never had a friend like me.

Gm **E♭7 D7 Gm**
Waahah.   Waahah.

E♭7 D7   **E♭7**   **D7 Gm**
You ain't never had a friend like me. *Ha!*

I'm Late

from Walt Disney's
ALICE IN WONDERLAND

Words by Bob Hilliard
Music by Sammy Fain

Melody:

I'm   late,   I'm   late

Verse

     Cm
I'm late, I'm late for a very important date.

    C   G7
No time to say hel - lo, goodbye,

              C
I'm late, I'm late, I'm late, I'm late,

    Cm
And   when I wave, I lose the time I save.

    Em   B7   Em   Am   Em
My fuzzy ears and whiskers took me too much time to shave.

G7   C   G7   C
I run and then I hop, hop, hop, I wish that I could fly.

     B7   Em   D7   G7
There's danger if I dare to stop and here's the reason why,

             Cm   D7
(You see.) I'm   overdue, I'm in a rabbit stew,

        C   G7
Can't even say good - bye, hello,

       C   F   C
I'm late, I'm late, I'm late.

© 1949 Walt Disney Music Company
Copyright Renewed
All Rights Reserved   Used by Permission

DISNEY

God Help the Outcasts

from Walt Disney's
THE HUNCHBACK OF NOTRE DAME

Music by Alan Menken
Lyrics by Stephen Schwartz

Melody:

I don't know if You can hear me ___

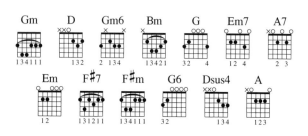

Verse 1

>   **Gm**   **D**
> *Esmerelda:* I don't know if You can hear me
>
> **Gm6**   **D**
> Or if You're even there.
>
> **Bm**   **G**
> I don't know if You would listen
>
> **Em7**   **A7** **D**
> To a gyp - sy's prayer.
>
> **Bm**   **Em**
> Yes, I know I'm just an outcast,
>
> **A7**   **F♯7** **Bm**
> I shouldn't speak to   You.
>
> **Gm6**   **D**   **F♯m**
> Still, I see Your face and won - der
>
> **A7**   **D Gm6 D Gm6**
> Were You once an outcast too?

© 1996 Wonderland Music Company, Inc. and Walt Disney Music Company
All Rights Reserved   Used by Permission

Chorus 1

D   G6
God help the outcasts, hungry from birth.

Em7   A7   Dsus4 D
Show them the mercy they don't   find on earth.

Bm   Em
God help my people, they look to You still.

Gm6   D   Em7   A7 D
God help the outcasts or nobod - y   will.

Verse 2

              Gm6   D   Gm6   Bm
Parishioners: I ask for wealth.   I ask for fame.

          G   A   D
I ask for glory to shine on my name.

F#7   Bm   G
  I ask for love I can pos - sess.

Bm   Em7   D   A
  I ask for God and His angels to bless me.

Outro

             D   G   G6
Esmeralda: I ask for nothing. I can get by,

Em7   A7   Dsus4 D
But I know so many less luck - y than I.

Bm   D   Em
Please help my peo - ple, the poor and downtrod.

Gm6   D   A7   Bm
I thought we all were the children of God.

Em7   D   A7   D Gm6 D Bm G A D
God help the outcasts, children of God.

Hakuna Matata

from Walt Disney Pictures' THE LION KING

Music by Elton John
Lyrics by Tim Rice

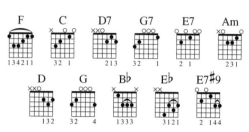

Chorus 1

           N.C.   **F**   **C**
Timon: Hakuna ma - tata…what a wonderful phrase!

                     F   **D7**   **G7**
Pumbaa: Hakuna ma - tata… ain't no passing craze.

             E7   **Am**   **C**   **F**   **D**
Timon: It means no worries for the rest ___ of your days.

                           C   **G**
Timon & Pumbaa: It's our problem-free phi - losophy.

           N.C.   **C**
Timon: Hakuna ma - tata.

Verse

                    Bb   **F**   **C**
Timon: Why, when he was a young wart - hog…

                  Bb   **F**   **C**
Pumbaa: When I was a young wart - hog!

              N.C.
Timon: Very nice. Pumbaa: Thanks.

           Eb   **F**
Timon: He found his aroma lacked a certain appeal.

           C   **G**
He could clear the savannah after ev'ry meal!

               Bb   **F**   **C**
Pumbaa: I'm a sensitive soul,   though I seem thick - skinned.

      Eb   **F**   **G**
And it hurt that my friends never stood down wind!

© 1994 Wonderland Music Company, Inc.
All Rights Reserved   Used by Permission

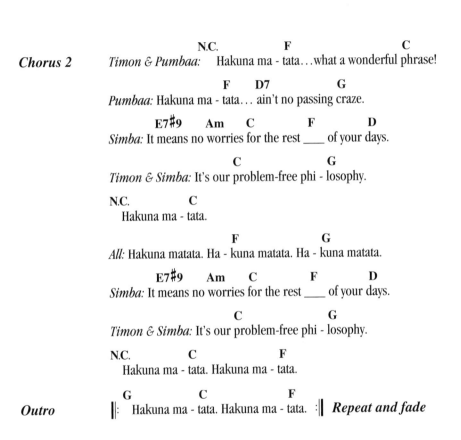

Chorus 2

N.C.   F   C
Timon & Pumbaa: Hakuna ma - tata...what a wonderful phrase!

           F   D7   G
Pumbaa: Hakuna ma - tata... ain't no passing craze.

     E7$\sharp$9   Am   C   F   D
Simba: It means no worries for the rest ___ of your days.

                   C   G
Timon & Simba: It's our problem-free phi - losophy.

N.C.   C
Hakuna ma - tata.

            F   G
All: Hakuna matata. Ha - kuna matata. Ha - kuna matata.

     E7$\sharp$9   Am   C   F   D
Simba: It means no worries for the rest ___ of your days.

                   C   G
Timon & Simba: It's our problem-free phi - losophy.

N.C.   C   F
Hakuna ma - tata. Hakuna ma - tata.

Outro

   G   C   F
‖: Hakuna ma - tata. Hakuna ma - tata. :‖ ***Repeat and fade***

He's a Tramp
from Walt Disney's LADY AND THE TRAMP
Words and Music by
Peggy Lee and Sonny Burke

Melody:

He's a tramp,   but they

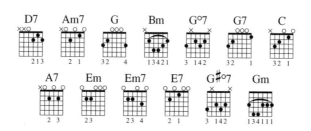

Verse 1

        D7   **Am7**   **D7**
He's a tramp, ___ but they love him.

  Am7   **G**   **D7**   **Am7**
Breaks a new heart ___ ev'ry - day.

      Bm   **D7**   **G**
He's a tramp, ___ they a - dore him

       G°7   **D7**   **G**
And I only hope he'll stay that way.

Verse 2

        D7   **Am7**   **D7**
He's a tramp, ___ he's a scoundrel,

  Am7   **G**   **D7**   **Am7**
He's a rounder, ___ he's a cad,

      Bm   **D7**   **G**
He's a tramp, ___ but I love him.

       G°7   **D7**   **G**
Yes, even I have got it pretty bad.

© 1952 Walt Disney Music Company
Copyright Renewed
All Rights Reserved   Used by Permission

GUITAR CHORD SONGBOOK

Bridge

        G7
You can never tell when he'll show up.

C   G7   C
He gives you plenty of trouble.

A7   Em
I guess he's just a no 'count pup.

Em7 E7   Am7 D7
But I wish that he were double.

Outro

             Am7   D7
He's a tramp, ____ he's a rover

Am7   G   G#°7   Am7
And there's nothing more to say.

             Bm D7   G
If he's a tramp, ____   he's a good one

     Gm   D7   G
And I wish that I could travel his way.

I Just Can't Wait to Be King

from Walt Disney Pictures' THE LION KING

Music by Elton John
Lyrics by Tim Rice

Melody:

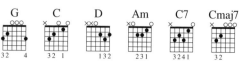

I'm gon-na be a might-y king,

G   C   D   Am   C7   Cmaj7

Intro   ‖: G |C G | |D :‖

Verse 1

                  G
Simba: I'm gonna be a mighty king, so enemies beware!
                                C   G
Zazu: Well, I've never seen a king of beasts with quite so little hair.

Simba: I'm gonna be the mane event, like no king was before.
        C   G
I'm brushing up on looking down. I'm working on my roar!

Chorus 1

               Am   G   D   N.C.
Zazu: Thus far, a rather unin - spiring thing.
             C7   D   G
Simba: Oh, I just can't wait to be king!
             C   G   N.C.
Zazu: You've rather a long way to go, young Master! If you think...

Bridge 1

                            C
Simba: No one saying "do this," *Zazu: Now when I said that I...*
                            Am
Simba: No one saying "be there," *Zazu: What I meant was that the...*
                            D
Simba: No one's saying "stop that," *Zazu: But what you don't realize...*
                            G
Simba: No one saying "see here." *Zazu: Now see here!*
             C   G   Am Cmaj7 D
Simba: Free to run a - round all   day,

Zazu: Well, that's definitely out.
             C7   D   G
Simba: Free to do it all my way!

© 1994 Wonderland Music Company, Inc.
All Rights Reserved Used by Permission

Verse 2
              G
Zazu: I think it's time that you and I arranged a heart to heart.

          C   G
Simba: Kings don't need advice from little hornbills, for a start.

Zazu: If this is where the monarchy is headed, count me out!
        C   G
Out of service, out of Africa. I wouldn't hang about.

Chorus 2
                  Am   G   D   N.C.
Zazu: This child is getting wildly out of wing.

             C7   D   G
Simba: Oh, I just can't wait to be king!

Bridge 2
                       C   Am
Simba: Ev'rybody look left. *Nala:* Ev'rybody look right.

                     D
Simba: Ev'rywhere you look I'm

                      G
Simba & Nala: Standing in the spotlight.

Zazu: Not yet.
                     C   G   Am   Cmaj7   D
Simba & Nala: Let ev'ry creature go ____ for broke and sing.

          C   G   Am   Cmaj7   D
Let's hear it in ____ the herd and on ____ the wing.

          C   G   Am   Cmaj7 D
It's gonna be ____ King Simba's fin - est   fling.

Outro-Chorus
             C7   D   G
Simba: Oh, I just can't wait to be king.

             C7   D   G
Oh, I just can't wait to be king.

             C7   D N.C.   G
Oh, I just can't wait   to be king!

I'm Wishing

from Walt Disney's
SNOW WHITE AND THE SEVEN DWARFS

Words by Larry Morey
Music by Frank Churchill

Melody:

It's so sad and lone - ly,

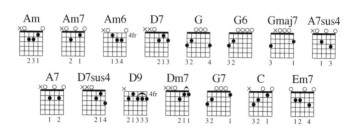

Verse

    Am   Am7   Am6
It's so sad and lonely, wishing well,

    Am   D7   G G6 Gmaj7 G6
Longing for some - one you never see.

    Am   Am7   Am6
Make him love me only, wishing well,

    A7sus4   A7   D7sus4 D7
Won't you grant this favor to me?

Chorus

        G6   D9   G6
I'm wishing for the one I love to find me to - day.

                  D9   G6
I'm hoping, and I'm dreaming of the nice things he'll say.

    Dm7   G7   C
Tell me, wishing well, will my wish come true?

    Em7   A7   D7
With your magic spell, won't you tell my loved one what to do?

        G6   D9   G
I'm wishing for the one I love to find me to - day.

Copyright © 1937 by Bourne Co. (ASCAP)
Copyright Renewed
International Copyright Secured   All Rights Reserved

If I Never Knew You

(Love Theme from POCAHONTAS)

from Walt Disney's POCAHONTAS

Music by Alan Menken
Lyrics by Stephen Schwartz

Melody:

If I nev - er know you,

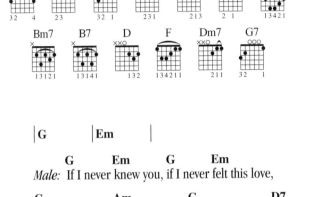

Intro | G | Em |

Verse 1

        G   **Em**   **G**   **Em**
Male: If I never knew you, if I never felt this love,

C   **Am**   **C**   **D7**
I would have no inkling of how precious life can be.

G   **Em**   **G**   **Em**   **E7**
And if I never held you, I would never have a clue

Am   **Cm**   **Em**   **Bm7** **C**
How, at last, I'd find in you   the missing part of me.

Am   **C**   **D7 Am**   **C D7**
  In this world so full of fear,   full of rage and lies,

Bm7   **B7**   **Em**   **C**   **D**
I can see ___ the truth so clear in your eyes, so dry your eyes.

Chorus 1

      G   **Em**
    And I'm so grateful to you.

G   **C**
I'd have lived my whole life through,

Am   **G**   **C**   **G**
Lost forev - er   if I never knew you.

© 1995 Wonderland Music Company, Inc. and Walt Disney Music Company
All Rights Reserved Used by Permission

Verse 2

        C   Am   C   Am
Female: If I never knew you, I'd be safe but half as real,

F   C   Dm7   F   G7
Never knowing I could feel ____ a love so strong and true.

Chorus 2

C   Am
I'm so grateful to you.

C   F
I'd have lived my whole life through,

Dm7   C F   G
Lost forev - er if I never knew you.

Bridge 1

       G   F   G
Male: I thought our love would be so beautiful.

         Em
Female: Somehow we'd make the whole world bright.

      G   F   C
Both: I never knew that fear and hate could be so strong,

        Am   Em   F
All they'd leave us were these whispers in the night,

     Dm7   Em   F   G7
But still my heart is saying we were right. *Female:* Oh.

Verse 3

      C Am   C   Am   F
Male: There's no moment I regret since the moment that we met.

C   Dm7   F   G Em F
If our time has gone too fast I've lived at last.

Bridge 2

      G   **F**
Both: I thought our love would be so beautiful,

Em
Somehow we'd make the whole world bright.

      G   **F**
Female: I thought our love would be so beautiful,

Em   **G** **C**
We'd turn the darkness in - to light,

      Dm7   **Em**   **F**
Both: And still my heart is saying we were right.

      Dm7
Male: We were right.

Chorus 2

       C   **Am**
Male: And if I never knew you,

C   **Em**   **F**
I'd have lived my whole life through

Dm7   **Em**   **F**
Empty as ____ the sky,

      Dm7   **Em** **F**
Both: Never know - ing why,

Am   **C** **F G7**   **C** **Am Dm7 G7 C**
Lost for - ever if I never knew you.

It's a Small World

from "it's a small world" at Disneyland Park and Magic Kingdom Park

Words and Music by Richard M. Sherman
and Robert B. Sherman

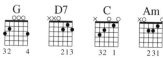

Verse

    G   **D7**
It's a world of laughter, a world of tears.

               G
It's a world of hopes and a world of fears.

There's so much that we share

      C   **Am**
That it's time we're a-ware.

D7   **G**
It's a small world after all.

        D7
It's a small world after all.

      G
It's a small world after all.

       C **Am**
It's a small world after all.

D7   **G**
It's a small, small world.

                D7
There is just one moon and one golden sun,

            G
And a smile means friendship to ev'ryone.

               C   **Am**
Though the mountains divide and the oceans are wide,

D7   **G**
It's a small world after all.

© 1963 Wonderland Music Company, Inc.
Copyright Renewed
All Rights Reserved   Used by Permission

Let's Go Fly a Kite
from Walt Disney's MARY POPPINS

Words and Music by Richard M. Sherman
and Robert B. Sherman

Melody:

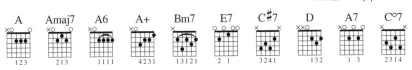

With — tup-pence for

A   Amaj7   A6   A+   Bm7   E7   C#7   D   A7   C°7

Verse 1

              A   Amaj7   A6
With tuppence for paper and strings

A+   A   A6   Bm7
  You can have your own set of wings.

E7   A   C#7   D   A
  With your feet on the ground you're a bird in flight

         Bm7   E7   A   A7
With your fist holding tight to the string of your kite. Oh!

Chorus 1

D   A
Let's go fly a kite up to the highest height!

E7   A   Bm7
Let's go fly a kite and send it

C°7   A   D
Soar - ing up through the atmosphere,

A
Up where the air is clear.

E7   A D A
Oh, let's go fly a kite!

Verse 2

E7   A   Amaj7   A6
  When you send it flying up there,

A+   A   A6   Bm7
  All at once you're lighter than air.

E7   A   C#7   D   A
  You can dance on the breeze over houses and trees,

         Bm7   E7   A   A7
With your fist holding tight to the string of your kite. Oh!

Chorus 2   *Repeat Chorus 1*

© 1963 Wonderland Music Company, Inc.
Copyright Renewed
All Rights Reserved   Used by Permission

Kiss the Girl

from Walt Disney's THE LITTLE MERMAID

Music by Alan Menken
Lyrics by Howard Ashman

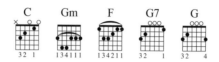

C   Gm   F   G7   G

Verse 1

    C
    There you see her sitting there across the way.   **Gm**

F   **C**
She don't got a lot to say, but there's something a - bout her.

    G7
And you don't know why, but you're dying to try.

     C
You wanna   kiss the girl.

                             Gm
Yes, you want her. Look at her, you know you do.

F   **C**
Possible she wants you, too. There is one way to ask her.

    G7
It don't take a word, not a single word,

      C
Go on and   kiss the girl.

Chorus 1

C   **F**
Sha, la, la, la, la, la, my oh my.

       C
Look like the boy too shy.

     G7
Ain't gonna   kiss the girl.

C   **F**
Sha, la, la, la, la, la, ain't that sad.

   G
Ain't it a shame, too bad.

    C
He gonna miss the girl.

© 1988 Wonderland Music Company, Inc. and Walt Disney Music Company
All Rights Reserved   Used by Permission

Verse 2

C   Gm
Now's your moment, floating in a blue lagoon.

F   C
Boy, you better do it soon, no time will be better.

           G7
She don't say a word and she won't say a word

           C
Until you   kiss the girl.

Chorus 2

C   F
 Sha, la, la, la, la, la, don't be scared.

               C   G7
You got the mood prepared, go on and   kiss the girl.

C   F
 Sha, la, la, la, la, la, don't stop now.

           G7   C
Don't try to hide it how you wanna   kiss the girl.

                   F
Sha, la, la, la, la, la, floating along.

                C   G7
And listen to the song, the song say   kiss the girl.

C   F
 Sha, la, la, la, la, la, the music play.

           G7   C
Do what the music say. You gotta   kiss the girl.

Outro

                  C
You've got to   kiss the girl. You wanna kiss the girl.

You've gotta kiss the girl. Go on and kiss the girl.

Lavender Blue
(Dilly Dilly)
from Walt Disney's SO DEAR TO MY HEART

Words by Larry Morey
Music by Eliot Daniel

Melody:

Lav - en - der blue,   dil - ly, dil - ly,

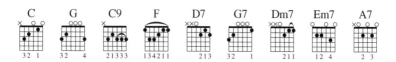

Verse 1

> C   G C9   F   C
> Lavender blue, dilly, dilly,   lavender green;
>
> F   C   F   D7   G7
> If I were king, dilly, dilly, I'd need a queen.
>
> C   G C9   F   C
> Who told me so, dilly, dilly,   who told me so?
>
> F   C   F   Dm7 G7   C
> I told my - self, dilly, dilly, I told ___ me so.
>
>   F
> If your dilly, dilly heart feels a dilly, dilly way
>
>   Em7 A7   Em7
> 'N' if you'll answer, "Yes,"
>
> A7 G
>   In a pretty little church on a dilly, dilly day
>
> D7   G7   C   G
> You'll be wed in a dilly, dilly dress of lavender blue,
>
> C9   F   C
> Dilly, dilly,   lavender green,
>
> F   C   F   Dm7   G7   C   F G7
> Then I'll be king, dilly, dilly and you'll be my queen.

© 1948 Walt Disney Music Company
Copyright Renewed
All Rights Reserved Used by Permission

Verse 2

```
        C      G    C9      F        C
Lavender blue, dilly, dilly,  lavender green;

F        C    F      D7        G7
If you were king, dilly, dilly, you'd need a queen.

C         G  C9      F           C
Who told me so, dilly, dilly,   who told me so?

F        C    F       Dm7  G7    C
I told my - self, dilly, dilly, I told ___ me so.

        F
If your dilly, dilly heart feels a dilly, dilly way

   Em7    A7     Em7
'N' if you'll answer, "Yes,"

A7    G
  In a pretty little church on a dilly, dilly day

D7          G7              C     G
I'll be wed in a dilly, dilly dress of lavender blue,

C9        F        C
Dilly, dilly,   lavender green,

F          C    F      Dm7  G7    C   F C
Then you'll be king, dilly, dilly and I'll be your queen.
```

Little April Shower

from Walt Disney's BAMBI

Words by Larry Morey
Music by Frank Churchill

Melody:

Drip, drip, drop, lit - tle   A - pril show - er,

C   G7   F   E   B7   A

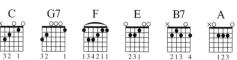

Verse 1

    C   G7   C   F
Drip, drip, drop, little April shower,

    C   F   C
Beating a tune as you fall all around.

            G7   C   F
Drip, drip, drop, little April shower,

    C   F   C
What can com - pare with your beautiful sound?

Bridge

    C   B7   E   A
Drip, drip, drop, when the sky is cloudy

    E   A   E
Your pretty music can brighten the day.

            B7   E   A
Drip, drip, drop, when the sun says "Howdy"

    E   B7   G7
You say "Good - bye" right a - way.

Verse 2

    C   G7   C   F
Drip, drip, drop, little April shower,

    E   F   C
Beating a tune ev'ry - where that you fall.

            G7   C   F
Drip, drip, drop, little April shower,

    C   F   C
I'm getting wet and I don't care at all.

Outro

    C   F   C   F
Drip! Drop! Drip! Drop!

    C   F   C
I'll never be a - fraid

                   G7   C
Of a good little gay little April sere - nade.

© 1942 Walt Disney Music Company and Wonderland Music Company, Inc.
Copyright Renewed
All Rights Reserved   Used by Permission

Look Through My Eyes

from Walt Disney Pictures' BROTHER BEAR

Words and Music by
Phil Collins

Melody:

There are   things   in ____

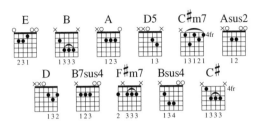

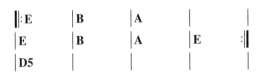

Intro

‖: E | B | A | | |
| E | B | A | E :‖
| D5 | | | |

Verse 1

    E   C#m7
There are things in   life you'll learn,

          E   Asus2
And   oh, in time you'll see,

E   C#m7
'Cause out there somewhere   it's all waiting

E   Asus2
If you keep be - lieving.

D   E   D
So don't run, don't hide.   It will be al - right.

                B7sus4
You'll see, trust me. ____ I'll be there watching over you.

© 2003 Walt Disney Music Company
All Rights Reserved   Used by Permission

Chorus 1

       E   Asus2 E
Just take a look through my eyes.

F#m7   E   C#m7
There's a better place somewhere out there.

Bsus4   E   Asus2 E
Ooh, just take a look through my eyes.

F#m7   E
Ev'rything changes.

C#m7   Bsus4   A
You'll be a - mazed what you'll find

      B   A   D5
If you look through my eyes.

Verse 2

E   C#m7
There will be times   on this journey,

E   Asus2
All you see is darkness,

E   C#m7
But out there somewhere   daylight finds you

E   Asus2
If you keep be - lieving.

D
So don't run, don't hide.

E   D
It will be al - right.

               B7sus4
You'll see, trust me. ____ I'll be there watching over you.

Chorus 2

    E   Asus2 E
Just take a look through my eyes.

F♯m7   E   C♯m7
 There's a better place somewhere out there.

Bsus4   E   Asus2 E
Ooh, just take a look through my eyes.

F♯m7   E
 Ev'rything changes.

C♯m7 Bsus4   A
You'll be a - mazed what you'll find

    B   A B7sus4
If you look through my eyes.

Chorus 3

    E   Asus2 E
Just take a look through my eyes.

F♯m7   E   C♯m7
 There's a better place somewhere out there.

Bsus4   E   Asus2 E
Ooh, just take a look through my eyes.

F♯m7   E
 Ev'rything changes.

C♯m7 Bsus4   A
You'll be a - mazed what you'll find

    B   A
If you look through my eyes.

Outro

    B
 Take a look through my, take a look through my,

         C♯
Take a look through my eyes.

The Lord Is Good to Me

from Walt Disney's MELODY TIME
from Walt Disney's JOHNNY APPLESEED

Words and Music by
Kim Gannon and Walter Kent

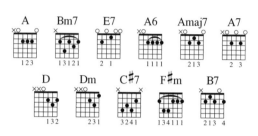

Verse 1

　　　　　　　A　　　　　　Bm7　E7　　A6　　　　　　　Bm7
The Lord is good to me,　　　and so I thank the Lord

E7　　A　　　　　Amaj7
　For givin' me the things I need,

　　A7　　　　　　　　　　D　　Dm
The sun and rain and an apple seed, yes,

A6　　　Bm7　E7　A Bm7　E7　A
He's been good　to　me.

Verse 2

Bm7　E7　A　　　A6　　　Bm7　E7　　A6　　　　　Bm7
　　I owe the Lord so much　　for ev'rything I see.

E7　　A　　　　　Amaj7
　I'm certain if it weren't for Him

　　　A7　　　　　D　　Dm
There'd be no apples on this limb, yes,

A6　　　Bm7　E7　A　D
He's been good　to　me.

© 1946 Walt Disney Music Company
Copyright Renewed
All Rights Reserved   Used by Permission

Bridge

    A D
Oh, here am I 'neath a blue, blue sky a-doin' as I please,

C♯7   F♯m   B7   E7
Singin' with my feathered friends, hummin' with the bees.

Verse 3

    A   Bm7 E7 A6 Bm7
I wake up ev'ry day as happy as can be

E7 A   Amaj7
Be - cause I know that with His care

  A7   D Dm
My apple trees they will still be there.

    A6   Bm7 E7 A D A
Oh, the Lord's been good to me.

Mickey Mouse March

from Walt Disney's THE MICKEY MOUSE CLUB

Words and Music by
Jimmie Dodd

Mick - ey   Mouse   Club!

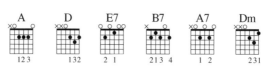

| A | D | E7 | B7 | A7 | Dm |

Intro
A   D   E7   A   D   E7
Mickey Mouse Club! Mickey Mouse Club!

Verse 1
A
Who's the leader of the club

B7   E7
That's made for you and me?

A   A7   D   Dm
M - I - C - K - E - Y

A   E7   A
M - O - U - S - E!

Verse 2
A
Hey, there! Hi, there! Ho, there!

B7   E7
You're as welcome as can be!

A   A7   D   Dm
M - I - C - K - E - Y

A   E7   A
M - O - U - S - E!

© 1955 Walt Disney Music Company
Copyright Renewed
All Rights Reserved   Used by Permission

Bridge

       D   **A**
Mickey Mouse! Mickey Mouse!

  B7   **E7**
For-ever let us hold our banner high!

(High! High! High!)

Verse 3

A
Come along and sing a song

  B7   **E7**
And join the jambo-ree!

A   **A7** **D**   **Dm**
M - I - C - K - E - Y

A   **E7**   **A**
M - O - U - S - E!

My Funny Friend and Me

from Walt Disney Pictures' THE EMPEROR'S NEW GROOVE

Lyrics by Sting
Music by Sting and David Hartley

In the qui - et time of eve - ning,

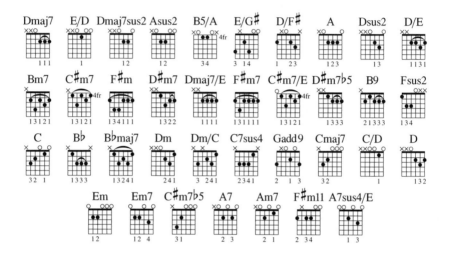

Intro

‖: Dmaj7   E/D |Dmaj7sus2   :‖

Verse 1

                  Asus2   B5/A   E/G♯
                  In the quiet time of the evening,

                  D/F♯   A   Dsus2
                  When the stars assume their pat - terns

                  Asus2   E/G♯
                  And the day has made his journey,

                  Dmaj7   D/E   Dmaj7
                  And we wonder just what happened to the life we knew,

                          Bm7 C♯m7   F♯m   D♯m7
                  Before the world changed, when not a thing I held was true.

                  Dmaj7   D/E
                  But you were kind to me,   and you reminded me

© 2000 Wonderland Music Company, Inc.
All Rights Reserved   Used by Permission

Verse 2

Asus2   B5/A E/G#
That the world is not my playground;
D/F#   A Dsus2
There are other things that mat - ter;
Asus2   E/G#
What is simple needs pro - tecting.
Dmaj7   D/E   Dmaj7 Bm7 C#m7
My illusions all would shatter, but you stayed in my cor - ner.
F#m   D#m7
The only world I knew was upside ___ down,
Dmaj7   Dmaj7/E
And now the world and me will know you carried me.
Asus2   E/G#
You see the patterns in the big sky;
Dmaj7   E/G#
Those constellations look like you and I.
F#m7   C#m7/E
Just like the patterns in the big sky,
D#m7♭5   B9
We could be lost; we could re - fuse to try.
    Dmaj7   Bm7 C#m7
But to have made it through in the dark night,
F#m   D#m7
Who would these lucky guys turn out to be,
Dmaj7   D/E   Asus2 E/G#
But that unusual blend of my funny friend and me.

Chorus 1

Asus2   E/G#
You see the patterns in the big sky;
Dmaj7   E/G#
Those constellations look like you and I.
F#m7   C#m7/E
Just like the patterns in the big sky,
D#m7♭5   B9
We could be lost; we could re - fuse to try.
    Dmaj7   Bm7 C#m7
But to have made it through in the dark night,
F#m   D#m7
Who would these lucky guys turn out to be,
Dmaj7   D/E   Asus2 E/G#
But that unusual blend of my funny friend and me.

Verse 3

Asus2   B5/A E/G♯
I'm not as clever as I thought I was.

D/F♯   A   Dsus2
I'm not the boy I used to be, be - cause

Asus2
You showed me something diff'rent;

        E/G♯
You showed ___ me something pure.

Dmaj7   D/E
I always seemed so certain, but I was real - ly never sure.

     Dmaj7   Bm7   C♯m7
But you stayed, and you called my name

F♯m   D♯m7
When others would have walked out on a lou - sy game.

Dmaj7   D/E   Fsus2
And look who made it through but your funny friend and you.

Outro-Chorus

              C B♭
You see the patterns in the big sky.

B♭maj7   C
Those constellations look like you and I.

Dm   Dm/C
That tiny planet and the bigger guy.

B♭maj7   C7sus4
I don't know whether I should laugh or cry.

Gadd9   D/F♯
Just like the pattern in the big sky, (We'll be together, ooh.)

Cmaj7   C/D D
We'll be together till the end of time.

Em   Em7
Don't know the answer or the reason why (We'll stick together.)

C♯m7♭5   A7
We'll stick together till the day we die.

Cmaj7   Am7   Bm7
If I have to do this all a second time,

Em7   C♯m7
I won't complain or make a fuss.

Cmaj7   C♯m7♭5
Who would the angel send,   but that unlikely blend

C/D
Of these two funny friends?

Gadd9   F♯m11 A7sus4/E D Cmaj7 C/D Gadd9
That's us.

Once Upon a Dream

from Walt Disney's SLEEPING BEAUTY

Words and Music by Sammy Fain and Jack Lawrence
Adapted from a Theme by Tchaikovsky

Melody:

I know you!

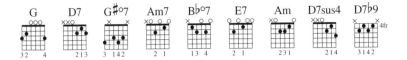

Verse

G
I know you!

          D7   **G#°7 Am7 D7**
I walked with you once up - on a dream.

G B♭°7 Am7
I know you!

    D7   **G**
The gleam in your eyes

    E7   **Am7**   **D7**
Is so fa - miliar a gleam.

          G
Yet, I know it's true

          Am7   **E7**   **Am**
That visions are seldom all they seem.

B♭°7 G   **B♭°7**
But if I know you,

    Am7   **D7**
I know what you'll do;

       G   **G#°7**   **E7**
You'll love me at once the way you did

Am7   **D7sus4 D7♭9 G**
Once up - on   a   dream.

© 1952 Walt Disney Music Company
Copyright Renewed
All Rights Reserved Used by Permission

Never Smile at a Crocodile

from Walt Disney's PETER PAN

Words by Jack Lawrence
Music by Frank Churchill

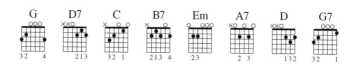

G   D7   C   B7   Em   A7   D   G7

Verse 1

      G   **D7 G**
Never smile at a crocodile,

          C   **G**
No, you can't get friendly with a crocodile.

B7   **Em**   **B7**   **Em**
Don't be taken in by his welcome grin,

          A7   **D**   **D7**
He's im - agining how well you'd fit with - in his skin.

G   **D7 G**
Never smile at a crocodile,

          C   **G**
Never tip your hat and stop to talk a while.

          C   **G**   **C**   **G**
Never run, walk a - way, say "Good - night" not "Good - day!"

          C   **G**   **D7 G**
Clear the aisle and never smile at Mister Croc - o - dile.

© 1952 Walt Disney Music Company
Copyright Renewed
All Rights Reserved   Used by Permission

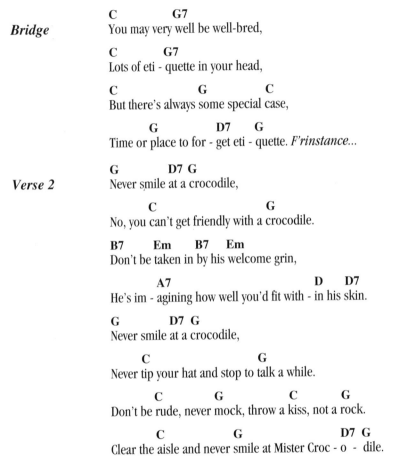

Bridge

C   G7
You may very well be well-bred,

C   G7
Lots of eti - quette in your head,

C   G   C
But there's always some special case,

G   D7   G
Time or place to for - get eti - quette. *F'rinstance...*

Verse 2

G   D7 G
Never smile at a crocodile,

C   G
No, you can't get friendly with a crocodile.

B7   Em   B7   Em
Don't be taken in by his welcome grin,

A7   D   D7
He's im - agining how well you'd fit with - in his skin.

G   D7 G
Never smile at a crocodile,

C   G
Never tip your hat and stop to talk a while.

C   G   C   G
Don't be rude, never mock, throw a kiss, not a rock.

C   G   D7 G
Clear the aisle and never smile at Mister Croc - o - dile.

Part of Your World

from Walt Disney's THE LITTLE MERMAID

Music by Alan Menken
Lyrics by Howard Ashman

Melody:

Look at this stuff. _   Is - n't it neat? _

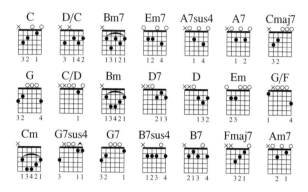

Verse

C   D/C
Look at this stuff. Isn't it neat?

C   D/C
Wouldn't you think my col - lection's complete?

Bm7   Em7
Wouldn't you think I'm the girl,

              A7sus4   A7
The girl who has ev'rything.

C   D/C
Look at this trove, treasures untold.

C   D/C
How many wonders can one cavern hold?

Bm7   Em7
Looking around here you'd think

              A7sus4
Sure, she's got ev'rything.

© 1988 Wonderland Music Company, Inc. and Walt Disney Music Company
All Rights Reserved   Used by Permission

Pre-Chorus

```
A7       Cmaj7              Bm7
I've got gadgets and gizmos a - plenty.

G       Em7                    A7sus4
I've got who-zits and what-zits ga - lore.

A7       Cmaj7                Bm7
You want thing-a-ma-bobs, I've got twenty.

G        Em7           A7sus4
But who cares? No big deal.

A7     C/D Bm C/D D7
I want more.
```

Chorus

```
G                   Bm7
I wanna be where the people are.

C              C/D        D
I wanna see, wanna see 'em danc - in',

Em                  Bm            C/D  D  D7
Walkin' around on those, what-d'-ya call 'em, oh feet.

G
Flippin' your fins you don't get too far.

C                  C/D          D
Legs are required for jumpin', danc - in'.

Em                 Bm       G        C/D
Strollin' along down the,   what's the word again,   street.

D7         G               G/F
   Up where they walk, up where they run,

                   C              Cm
Up where they stay all day in the sun.

           G             C/D  D       G
Wanderin' free, wish I could be    part of that world.
```

            C   D/C   Bm
What would I give if I could live outta these waters.

Em   C   D/C   Bm
  What would I pay to spend a day warm on the sand?

G7sus4 G7   C   D/C
  Betcha on land they under - stand.

            B7sus4   B7   Em
Bet they don't reprimand ___ their daugh - ters.

Em7   A7sus4 A7   A7sus4
  Bright young women,   sick of swimmin',

A7   Fmaj7 C/D D C/D
Ready to stand.

         D   G
  And ready to know what the people know.

Cmaj7   C/D   D7
Ask 'em my questions and get some an - swers.

Em   Bm   G   Am7
What's a fire, and why does it, what's the word,   burn?

D7   G
  When's it my turn?

        G/F   C   Cm
Wouldn't I love, love to ex - plore that shore up a - bove,

N.C.   G
Out of the sea.

           C/D D7   G
Wish I could be   part of that world.

The Siamese Cat Song
from Walt Disney's LADY AND THE TRAMP

Words and Music by
Peggy Lee and Sonny Burke

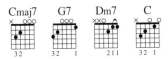

Verse 1

Cmaj7
We are Siamese if you please.

                    G7
We are Siamese if you don't please.

Dm7
We are former residents of Siam.

G7   C   G7 C
There are no finer cats than we am.

Verse 2

Cmaj7
We are Siamese with very dainty claws.

                    G7
Please observing paws containing dainty claws.

Dm7
Now we lookin' over our new domicile.

G7   C   G7 C
If we like we stay for maybe quite a while.

© 1953 Walt Disney Music Company
Copyright Renewed
All Rights Reserved   Used by Permission

A Pirate's Life
from Walt Disney's PETER PAN

Words by Ed Penner
Music by Oliver Wallace

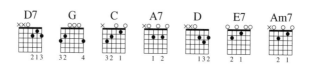

Verse 1

D7 G   C   G
Oh, a pirate's life is a wonderful life,

A7   D
A-roving over the sea.

E7   Am7   D7
Give me a career as bucca - neer,

     G   D7   G
It's the life of a pirate for me!

D7   G   D7   G
Oh! The life of a pirate for me!

Verse 2

D7 G   C   G
Oh, a pirate's life is a wonderful life,

    A7   D
With - out a care to be - hold.

E7   Am7   D7
You carry a gun and a jug of rum

     G   D7   G
And your pockets are loaded with gold!

D7   G   D7   G
Oh! Your pockets are loaded with gold!

© 1951 Walt Disney Music Company
Copyright Renewed
All Rights Reserved   Used by Permission

Verse 3

D7 G   C   G
Oh, a pirate's life is a wonderful life,

  A7   D
You find adventure and sport.

  E7   Am7   D7
But live ev'ry minute for all that's in it,

  G   D7   G
The life of a pirate is short!

D7   G   D7   G
Oh! The life of a pirate is short!

Verse 4

D7 G   C   G
Oh, a pirate's life is a wonderful life,

  A7   D
But not forever they say.

      E7   Am7   D7
When your neck's in a noose and you can't get loose,

    G   D7   G
For the life of a pirate you'll pay!

D7   G   D7   G
Oh! The life of a pirate you'll pay!

Reflection
from Walt Disney Pictures' MULAN

Music by Matthew Wilder
Lyrics by David Zippel

Melody:

Look at me,   you may think you see __

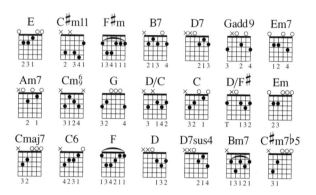

Verse 1

    E   **C♯m11**   **F♯m**
Look at me, you may think you see who I ____ really am,

               E   **B7**
But you'll never know me.

    E   **C♯m11**   **D7**
Ev'ry day it's as if I play a part.

Gadd9   **Em7**   **Am7**
Now I see if I wear a mask I can fool the world,

Cm⁶₉   **G**
But I cannot fool my heart.

Chorus 1

    G   **Em7**
Who is that girl I see

D/C   **C**   **Cm⁶₉**
Staring straight back at me?

G   **D/F♯** **Em** **G**   **Cmaj7 C6**
When will   my ____ re - flection show

Cm⁶₉   **G**   **Em7**
  Who I am in - side?

© 1998 Walt Disney Music Company
All Rights Reserved   Used by Permission

Verse 2

   E   C#m11   F#m
I am now in a world where I have to hide my heart

             B7
And what I be - lieve in.

   Gadd9   Em7   Am7
But somehow I will show the world what's in - side my heart,

   Cm§   G
And be loved for who I am.

Chorus 2

   G   Em7
Who is that girl I see

   D/C   C   Cm§
Staring straight back at me?

   G   D/F# Em G   Cmaj7 C6
Why is   my ___ re - flection someone

   F   D
I don't know?

   G   Em7   D/C   C Cm§
Must I pre - tend that I'm someone else for all time?

   G   D/F# Em G   Cmaj7   Cm§
When will   my ___ re - flection show who I am?

Pre-Chorus

      C   Em7   Am7   D7sus4
In - side, there's a heart that must be free to fly,

     Em7   Bm7   Am7   Cm§
That burns with a need to know the reason why.

Chorus 3

   G   Em7
Why must we all conceal

   D/C   C   Cm§
What we think, how we feel?

   G   D/F# Em G   Cmaj7 C6
Must there be ___ a secret me

     F   D
I'm forced to hide?

   G   Em7   D/C   C Cm§
I won't pre - tend that I'm someone else for all time.

   G   D/F# Em G   Cmaj7
When will   my ___ re - flection show

   Cm§   Em Em7 C#m7♭5
Who I am in - side?

   G   D/F# Em G   Cmaj7 C6
When will   my ___ re - flection show

   Cm§   G Em7 G
   Who I am in - side?

Shrimp Boats

Words and Music by
Paul Mason Howard and Paul Weston

Melody:

Shrimp boats   is   a - com - in',

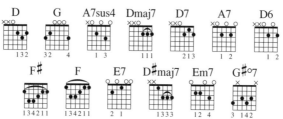

Chorus 1

    D   G   D   A7sus4 D
Shrimp boats is a - comin', their sails are in   sight.

                      G   D   A7sus4 D
Shrimp boats is a - comin', there's dancin' to - night.

Why don't cha hurry, hurry, hurry home,

Why don't cha hurry, hurry, hurry home? (Look, here the)

                      G   D   A7sus4 D
Shrimp boats is a - comin', there's dancin' to - night.

Verse 1

    Dmaj7 D7 G
They go   to sea

        D   A7sus4 D
With the eve - ning   tide

        A7sus4   A7   D
And their womenfolk wave their good - bye.

Dmaj7 D6 Dmaj7 D6
Ill _____ sant   vas,

Dmaj7 D6 Dmaj7 D6
There _____ they   go.

D   G   F# F
While the Lou'sian - a   moon

E7   D#maj7 D Em7 G#°7
Floats on   high,

D   G   F# F
And they wait for the day

E7 D#maj7 D
They can   cry.

© 1951 Walt Disney Music Company
Copyright Renewed 1979 Walt Disney Music Company and Hanover Music Corporation
All Rights Reserved   Used by Permission

Chorus 2	*Repeat Chorus 1*
Verse 2	**D Dmaj7 D7** Hap - py the days
	D A7sus4 D While they're mending the nets
	A7sus4 A7 D 'Till once more they ride high out to sea.
	Dmaj7 D6 Dmaj7 D6 Ill _____ sant vas,
	Dmaj7 D6 Dmaj7 D6 There ____ they go.
	D G F♯ Then how lonely the
	F E7 D♯maj7 D Em7 G♯°7 Long nights will be,
	D G F♯ F 'Till that wonder - ful day
	E7 D♯maj7 D When they see…
Chorus 3	*Repeat Chorus 1*

A Spoonful of Sugar
from Walt Disney's MARY POPPINS
Words and Music by Richard M. Sherman
and Robert B. Sherman

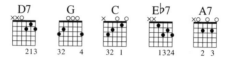

Verse 1

       G
In ev'ry job that must be done

There is an element of fun.

                         D7
You find the fun and snap the job's a game.

      C   **E♭7**
And ev'ry task you under-take

     G   **A7**
Be-comes a piece of cake,

      D7
A lark! A spree!

     A7   **D7**
It's very clear to see

© 1963 Wonderland Music Company, Inc.
Copyright Renewed
All Rights Reserved   Used by Permission

Chorus 1
    A7   D7   **G**
That a spoonful of sugar helps the medicine go down,

        D7   **G**
The medicine go down, medicine go down.

    A7   D7   **G**
Just a spoonful of sugar helps the medicine go down

              D7   G   D7
In a most de-lightful way.

Verse 2
              G
A robin feathering his nest

Has very little time to rest

                            D7
While gathering his bits of twine and twig.

                C   **E♭7**
Though quite in-tent in his pur-suit

    G   **A7**
He has a merry tune to toot.

          D7   **A7**   **D7**
He knows a song will move the job a-long.

    A7
For a...

Chorus 2   *Repeat Chorus 1*

Supercalifragilisticexpialidocious

from Walt Disney's MARY POPPINS

Words and Music by Richard M. Sherman
and Robert B. Sherman

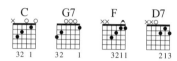

Chorus 1

C   G7
Supercalifragilisticexpiali-docious!

               C
Even though the sound of it is something quite a-trocious,

                 F
If you say it loud enough you'll always sound pre-cocious.

      C   G7   C
Supercali-fragilistic-expiali-docious!

Bridge

C   G7
Um diddle diddle diddle, um diddle ay!

C   G7
Um diddle diddle diddle, um diddle ay!

Verse

   C   G7
Be-cause I was afraid to speak when I was just a lad,

              C
Me father gave me nose a tweak and told me I was bad.

                F
But then one day I learned a word that saved me achin' nose,

D7   G7
The biggest word you ever 'eard and this is 'ow it goes! Oh!

Chorus 2   **Repeat Chorus 1**

© 1963 Wonderland Music Company, Inc.
Copyright Renewed
All Rights Reserved   Used by Permission

That's How You Know
from Walt Disney Pictures' ENCHANTED

Music by Alan Menken
Lyrics by Stephen Schwartz

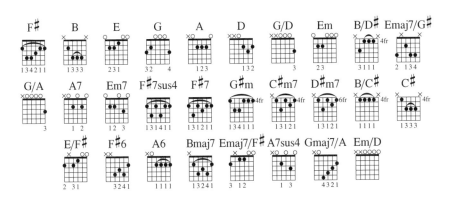

Intro

N.C.
How does she know you love her?

How does she know she's yours?

Refrain

(How does she know that you love her?)

How do you show her you love her?

How does she know that you really, really, truly love her?

How does she know that you love her?

How do you show her you love her?

F♯　B　E　G　A
How does she know that you real - ly,　really, truly love her?

© 2007 Wonderland Music Company, Inc. and Walt Disney Music Company
All Rights Reserved　Used by Permission

Verse 1

D G/D   D A D G/D Em A
It's not e - nough to take the one you love for granted.

D   G/D   A F♯ B B/D♯ E
You must re - mind her, or she'll be in - clined to say:

Chorus 1

Emaj7/G♯ G/A A7 D G/D Em7
 "How do I know

G/A A7 D   G/D Em7
He _____ loves me?

 G/A A7 D G/D Em7
How do I know

F♯7sus4 F♯7 B B/D♯ G♯m
He's _____ mine?"

B   E F♯ B   B/D♯
 Well, does he leave a little note

  E   C♯m7   F♯7
To tell you you are on his mind?

B   B/D♯ E   C♯m7   F♯7
Send you yellow flowers when the sky is gray? Hey!

D♯m7   G♯m B/C♯   C♯
He'll find a new way to show you a little bit ev'ry day.

E/F♯ F♯6 E/F♯ F♯6 E/F♯ F♯6
That's how you know,

G/A A6 G/A A6 N.C.
That's how you know he's your love.

Interlude 1

| D | | | |

| | | B Bmaj7 E |Emaj7/F♯ G/A A7 |

Refrain

D   G/D Em7   G/A A7
 (You've got to show her you need her,

D   G/D Em7   G/A A7
Don't treat her like a mind - read - er!

D   G/D Em7   F♯7sus4 F♯7
Each day do something to lead   her

B B/D♯ E Emaj7/G♯ G/A A7
To be - lieve you   love her.)

Verse 2

D   G/D   Em7   G/A A7 D
Ev'rybody wants to live happily ev - er   after.

     G/D Em7   G/A A7
(You've got to show her you need her.)

D   G   Em7   F♯7   B B/D♯ E
Ev'rybody wants to know ___ their true love is true.

Chorus 2

Emaj7/G♯ G/A A7 D   G/D Em7
How   do   you know

G/A A7 D   G/D Em7
He ____ loves you?

       G/A A7   D G/D
How do   you know

F♯7sus4 F♯7 B   B/D♯ G♯m
He's _____ yours?

B   E   F♯ B   B/D♯
Well, does he take you out dancing

E   C♯m7   F♯7
Just so he can hold you close?

B   B/D♯   E   C♯m7   F♯7
Dedicate a song with words meant just for you? Ooh!

D♯m7   G♯m B/C♯   C♯
He'll find his own way to tell you with the little things he'll do.

E/F♯ F♯6 E/F♯ F♯6 E/F♯ F♯6
That's how you   know,

G/A A6 G/A A7sus4 N.C.
That's how you   know   he's your love.

Interlude 2 | D | | | |
                    | | | B B/D♯ E |

Chorus 3
    Emaj7/G♯ G/A A7 D   G/D Em7
    That's   how you know

    G/A A7 D   G/D Em7
    He _____ loves you.

       G/A A7   D G/D Em7
    That's how you know

    F♯7sus4 F♯7 B B/D♯ G♯m
    It's _____ true.

    B   E   F♯ B   B/D♯
     Be - cause he'll wear your fav'rite color

    E   C♯m7   F♯7
    Just so he can match your eyes.

    B   B/D♯ E   C♯m7 F♯7
    Plan a private picnic by the fire's glow, oh.

    D♯m7   G♯m B/C♯   C♯
    His heart'll be yours for - ever,   something ev'ry day will show.

    E/F♯ F♯6 E/F♯ F♯6   E/F♯ F♯6
    That's how you   know,

    G/A A6 G/A A6
    That's how you   know,

    E/F♯ F♯6 E/F♯   F♯6 E/F♯ F♯6
    (That's how you   know,)

    G/A A6 G/A A6
    That's how you know.

    E/F♯   F♯6 E/F♯   F♯6 E/F♯ F♯6
    (That's how you   know,)

    G/A A6 G/A Gmaj7/A N.C.
    That's how you   know   he's your love.

Outro   (That's how she knows that you love her.

                                                  D
            That's how you show her   you love her.)
                                      That's how you   know.
                 G   **D**   **A**
            (You've got to show her you need her.

            D   **G**   **G/A** **A7** **D**
               Don't treat her like a mind   read - er.)
                                      That's how you   know.
                 G   **Em7**   **G/A** **A7**
            (How do you know that you love her?

            D   **G/D**   **Em7**   **G/A** **A7**   **D**
               That's how you know that you love her.)
                                   He's   your _____ love.

                      G/D   **Em7**   **G/A** **A7** **Em/D** **D**
            It's not e - nough to take the one you love for grant - ed!)

DISNEY   **87**

That's What Friends Are For
(The Vulture Song)
from Walt Disney's THE JUNGLE BOOK

Words and Music by Richard M. Sherman
and Robert B. Sherman

Melody:

We're your friends, _____ we're your

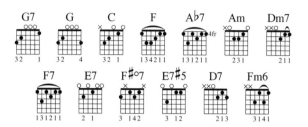

Intro

         G7
We're your friends, we're your friends,

                G
We're your friends to the bitter end.

Verse 1

G7   **C**   **F**   **A♭7 C**
When you're a - lone, (When you're a - lone.)

         Am   **Dm7 Am** **F7 Am**
Who comes a - round (Who comes a - round?)

G7   **C** **F**   **A♭7 C**
To pluck you up (To pluck you up.)

         Am   **Dm7 Am F7 Am**
When you are down; (When you are down.)

   G7   **C**   **E7**
And when you're outside, looking in,

             F   **F♯°7**
Who's there to open the door?

C   **G7**   **C**
That's what friends are for!

© 1965 Wonderland Music Company, Inc.
Copyright Renewed
All Rights Reserved Used by Permission

Verse 2

        C   **F**   **A♭7** **C**
Who hovers near, (Who hov - ers near?)

             Am   **Dm7** **Am** **F7** **Am**
Who are your chums (Who are   your chums?)

      G7   **C**   **F**   **A♭7** **C**
Pre - pared to pounce (Prepared to   pounce.)

            Am   **Dm7** **Am** **F7** **Am**
When danger comes; (When dan - ger comes.)

      G7   **C**   **E7**   **F**   **F♯°7**
Who's always eager to ex - tend a friendly claw?

C   **G7**   **C**
That's what friends are for!

Bridge

             E7   **Am**
And when you're lost in dire need,

       E7 **E7♯5** **Am**
Who's at your side at   lightning speed?

    D7   **G**
We're friends with ev'ry creature comin' down the pike.

         D7   **G7**   **D7** **G7**
In fact we've never met an animal we didn't like. Didn't like.

Outro

        C   **F**   **A♭7** **C**
So you can see (So you can   see.)

            Am   **Dm7** **Am** **F7** **Am**
We're friends in need. (We're friends in need.)

      G7   **C**   **F**   **A♭7** **C**
And friends in need (And friends in   need.)

            Am **Dm7** **Am** **F7** **Am**
Are friends in - deed. (Are   friends in - deed.)

      G7   **C**   **E7**   **F** **F♯°7** **F** **F♯°7**
We'll keep you safe in the jungle for - ev - er - more!

C   **G7**   **C** **Fm6** **C**
That's what friends are for!

These Are the Best Times

from Walt Disney Productions' SUPERDAD

Words and Music by
Shane Tatum

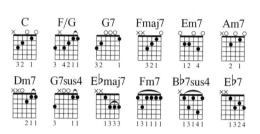

Verse 1

    C   F/G G7
These are the best   times,

    C   Fmaj7   Em7
The moments we can't let slip a - way.

Am7   **Dm7**
Life's little game we play,

G7sus4   **G7**   **C Fmaj7**
Living from day to day.

Verse 2

    C   F/G G7
But once in a life - time,

    C   Fmaj7   Em7
A minute like this is ours to share.

   Am7   **Dm7**
Re - member the moments well,

   G7sus4
For moments like these are...

© 1973 Wonderland Music Company, Inc.
Copyright Renewed
All Rights Reserved   Used by Permission

Bridge

     E♭maj7   Fm7   B♭7sus4
Rare as dreams and golden rainbows,

     E♭7   Fm7   B♭7sus4   Em7
 Soft as nights when summer wind blows by.

       Am7   Dm7
To - gether we laugh and cry,

       G7sus4   G7   C
To - gether we'll learn to fly.

Outro-Verse

                    F/G G7
Come take my hand,

     C   Fmaj7   Em7
 Together we'll cross the timeless sands,

     Am7   Dm7 G7sus4 G7   C
Chasing the endless sun,   living our lives as one.

This Is Me
from the Disney Channel Original Movie CAMP ROCK

Words and Music by
Adam Watts and Andy Dodd

I've al-ways been the kind _ of girl _

Am7   F5   Gsus4   Dm7   Am   F

C   Dm   G   G5   C5   C/E

Intro

|Am7   F5 |Gsus4   Dm7 |

Verse 1

    Am7   F5   Gsus4   Dm7
I've always been the kind of girl that hid my face,

    Am7   F5 Gsus4   Dm7
So a - fraid to tell the world what I've got to say.

   Am   F   C   Dm
But I have this dream bright inside of me,

    Am F   C Dm   F
I'm gonna let it show. It's time ___ to let you know,

    G
To let you know.

Chorus 1

     F   C
This is real, this is me,

    G   Am
I'm exact - ly where I'm sup - posed to be, now.

F   C G
 Gonna let the light ___ shine on me.

    Am   F   C   G
Now I've found who I am, ___ there's no way to hold it in.

Dm7   F
No more hiding who I want to be,

G   Am7 F5
 This is me.

© 2008 Walt Disney Music Company
All Rights Reserved   Used by Permission

Verse 2

```
            C  G5  C5    Am           F
               Do you know what it's like

            C        Dm
         To feel so in the dark,

            Am        F        C            Dm
         To dream about a life where you're the shining star?

            Am     F            C          Dm
         Even though it seems like it's ___ too far a - way.

            Am       F         C
         I have to be - lieve in myself.

            Dm        F
         It's the only way.
```

Chorus 2

```
                F          C
         This is real, this is me,

                  G              Am
         I'm exact - ly where I'm sup - posed to be, now.

         F                   C  G
            Gonna let the light ___ shine on me.

                  Am           F          C           G
         Now I've found who I am, ___ there's no way to hold it in.

         Dm7                       F
         No more hiding who I want to be,

         G        Am  F  C  Dm  Am  F
            This is me.
```

Bridge

```
         G              F              C
         You're the voice ___ I hear inside my head,

           G
         The reason that I'm singing.

                      F        C              G      Am7
         I need to find ___ you,    I've got to find ___ you.

         F                      C              G
         You're the missing piece I need, the song ___ inside of me.

         Am7        Dm                    G
         I need to find ___ you. I've got to find ___ you.
```

Chorus 3

```
              F        C
         This is real, this is me,

                 G                  Am
         I'm exact - ly where I'm sup - posed to be, now.

         F                    C  G
            Gonna let the light ___ shine on me.

                  Am            F          C            G
         Now I've found who I am, ___ there's no way to hold it in.

         Dm7                        F  G
         No more hiding who I want to be, ___    this is me.
```

Outro

```
         F                    C
         You're the missing piece ___ I need,

            Gsus4          G
         The song ___ inside of me.

                       F              C
         You're the voice ___ I hear inside ___ my head,

            Gsus4                Am
         The reason that I'm sing - ing.

                       F          C          G
         Now I've found ___ who I am, ___ there's no way to hold it in.

         Dm7                        F  G       F  C/E  G  Am  F
         No more hiding who I want to be, ___    this is me.
```

The Unbirthday Song

from Walt Disney's ALICE IN WONDERLAND

Words and Music by Mack David,
Al Hoffman and Jerry Livingston

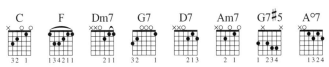

Sta - tis - tics prove,   prove that you've

C   F   Dm7   G7   D7   Am7   G7#5   A°7

Verse 1

              C   F   Dm7 G7
Sta - tistics prove, prove that you've one   birthday,

                    C
One birthday ev'ry year.

                                F   C   Dm7 G7
But there are three hundred and sixty - four un - birthdays,

D7   Am7   D7   G7
That is why we're gathered here to cheer.

Chorus 1

G7#5 C
A   very merry un-birthday to you, to you.

                             Dm7 G7   Dm7
A very merry un-birthday to you, _____ to you.

G7   C   Dm7
It's great to drink to someone and I guess that you will do.

A°7 G7   C A°7 G7
A very merry un-birthday to you.

Chorus 2

G7#5 C
A   very merry un-birthday to me, to who?

                           Dm7 G7   Dm7
A very merry un-birthday to me. _____ To you?

G7   C   Dm7
Let's all congratulate me with a present, I a - gree.

A°7 G7
A very merry un-birthday, a very merry un-birthday,

                                G7#5 C
A very merry un-birthday to   me.

© 1948 Walt Disney Music Company
Copyright Renewed
All Rights Reserved   Used by Permission

Under the Sea
from Walt Disney's THE LITTLE MERMAID

Music by Alan Menken
Lyrics by Howard Ashman

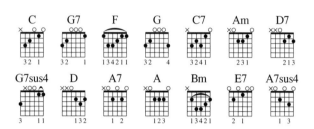

Verse 1

      C   G7   C
The seaweed is always greener

          G7   C
In somebody else's lake.

            G7   C
You dream about going up there.

         G7   C
But that is a big mis - take.

F   C
Just look at the world around you,

G7   C
Right here on the ocean floor.

F   C
Such wonderful things surround you.

G7   C
What more is you lookin' for?

© 1988 Wonderland Music Company, Inc. and Walt Disney Music Company
All Rights Reserved   Used by Permission

Chorus 1

N.C.   **F**   **C**   **G7**
Under the sea,   under the sea.

C   **F**   **G**
Darlin' it's better down where it's wetter.

          C
Take it from me.

C7   **F**
Up on the shore they work all day.

G   **Am**
Out in the sun they slave away.

D7   **F**   **G7**   **C G7 C G7 C**
While we de - votin' full time to floatin' under the sea.

Verse 2

C   **G7**   **C**
Down here all the fish is happy

           G7   **C**
As off through the waves they roll.

         G7   **C**
The fish on the land ain't happy.

          G7   **C**
They sad 'cause they in the bowl.

F   **C**
But fish in the bowl is lucky,

G7   **C**
They in for a worser fate.

F   **C**
One day when the boss gets hungry

G7   **C**
Guess who gon' be on the plate.

Chorus 2

N.C.   F C   G7
Under the sea,   under the sea.

C   F   G7   C
Nobody beat us, fry us and eat us in fricas - see.

C7   F
We what the land folks love to cook.

G   Am
Under the sea we off the hook.

D7   F   G7
We got no troubles, life is the bubbles

          F C   G7
Under the sea.   Under the sea.

Verse 3

C   F   G   G7 C
Since life is sweet here we got the beat here nat - ural - ly.

C7   F   G   Am
Even the sturgeon an' the ray   they get the urge 'n start to play.

D7   F   G7   C
We got the spirit, you got to hear it under the sea.

Bridge

G7 C   G   C
        The newt ___ play the flute. The carp ___ play the harp.

          G   C
The plaice ___ play the bass. And they ___ soundin' sharp.

        F   C
The bass ___ play the brass. The chub ___ play the tub.

       G   G7   C
The fluke ___ is the duke of soul.

       G   G7   C
The ray ___ he can play. The lings ___ on the strings.

        G   G7   C
The trout ___ rockin' out. The black - fish she sings.

         F   C
The smelt ___ and the sprat they know ___ where it's at.

     G   G7   C
An' oh, that blowfish blow.

Interlude

```
|F       |C        |G7    |C      |
|F       |G7       |C     |       |
|F       |G7       |Am    |D7     |
|F       |G7sus4 G7|C     |G7  C  |
|        |G7   C   |D     |A7  D  |
|        |         |      |
```

Chorus 3

        G D   A7
Under the sea,   under the sea.

D   G   A7   D
When the sar - dine begin the be - guine it's music to me.

D7   G
What do they got, a lot of sand.

A   Bm   E7
We got a hot crustacean band.

             G   A7   D
Each little clam here know how to jam ___ here under the sea.

A7 D   G   A   D
Each little slug here cuttin' a rug here under the sea.

A7 D   G   A
Each little snail here know how to wail here.

             Bm   E7
That's why it's hotter under the water.

             G   A7sus4
Yeah, we in luck here down in the muck here

    A7   D A7 D A7 D
Un - der the sea.

Westward Ho, The Wagons!

from Walt Disney's WESTWARD HO, THE WAGONS!

Words by Tom Blackburn
Music by George Bruns

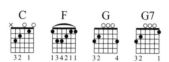

Verse

       C   F
There's magic in the wind, and a brightness in the sky.

       C
There's a promised land a-waitin'

             G   C
And we'll get there bye and bye.

Westward Ho, the wagons!

     F   C
Always westward roll.

                           G7   C
Westward roll the wagons for Ore - gon's our goal.

© 1955 Wonderland Music Company, Inc.
Copyright Renewed
All Rights Reserved   Used by Permission

Where the Dream Takes You
from Walt Disney Pictures' ATLANTIS: THE LOST EMPIRE

Lyrics by Diane Warren
Music by Diane Warren and
James Newton Howard

They'll try to hold _ you   back,

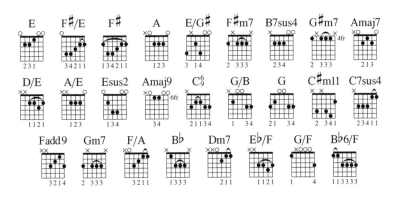

Intro

‖: E | F♯/E :‖

Verse 1

E   F♯
They'll try to hold you back,

E   F♯
They will say you're wrong,

A   E/G♯
But they will never understand, no,

F♯m7   B7sus4
The journey that you're on.

Verse 2

E   F♯
They'll try to change your mind,

E   F♯
They'll try to change your heart,

          A   E/G♯   F♯m7
Oh yeah,   but they will never understand who ___ you are.

© 2001 Walt Disney Music Company
All Rights Reserved   Used by Permission

Chorus 1

G#m7   Amaj7   E/G#
And you still believe (Still believe.)

F#m7   B7sus4
And you know (And you know.) You must go (You must go.)

      E
Where the dream takes you.(Where the dream takes your heart,)

      F#m7   E/G#
Where the heart longs to be (Your dream will lead you on.)

A   E/G#   B7sus4
When you fin'lly find that place you'll find all you need,

        D/E   A/E   Esus2
Where the dream takes you. ___ *(Where the dream takes you.)*

Verse 3

E   F#
There's something in your soul

E   F#
That won't be de - nied.

A   E/G#   F#m7
It's the faith to dream that keeps the dream alive.

Chorus 2

G#m7   Amaj7   E/G#
So you still believe (Still believe.)

F#m7   B7sus4
And you know (And you know.) You must go (You must go.)

      E
Where the dream takes you.(Where the dream takes your heart,)

      F#m7   E/G#
Where the heart longs to be (Your dream will lead you on.)

A   E/G#   B7sus4
When you fin'lly find that place you'll find all you need,

        D/E
Where the dream takes you.

Bridge

                             Amaj9
Go where your heart is meant ___ to be

C$\frac{6}{9}$
And you may find (You may find.)

   G/B
Some - body there (Somebody there.)

        G   F#m7 E
Someone to share your   dream.

                       F#m7
(Where your dream takes your heart,

        E/G#
Your dream will lead you on.)

A   **C#m11**
  When you fin'lly find that place,

   F#m7   **B7sus4**
You'll ___ find all you need.

Outro-Chorus

C7sus4   **Fadd9**
  Where the dream leads you. (Your dream will lead you home.)

   Gm7   **F/A**
Far as your ___ heart can see. (Your dream will lead you on.)

Bb   **Dm7**
  There's a world that waits for you.

   Gm7 Dm7   **C7sus4**
You're not alone,   you'll find your home.

    Eb/F   **Bb**
(Where the dream takes you.) Try to change your mind,

    Fadd9
(Where the dream takes you.) Try to change your heart.

    G/F
(Where the dream takes you.)

     Bb6/F
Why don't you just go *where the dream takes you.*

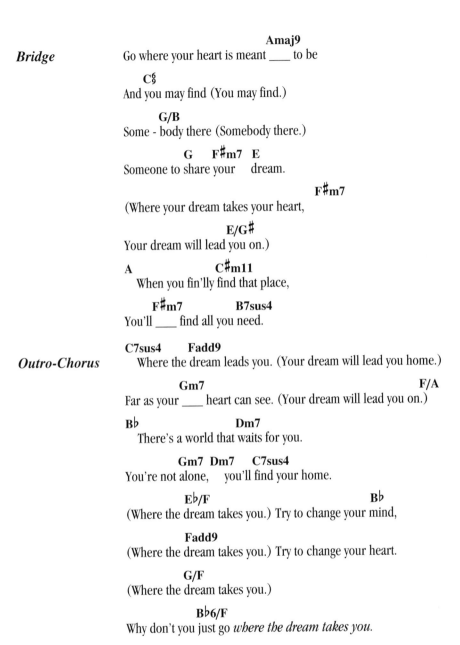

A Whale of a Tale

from Walt Disney's 20,000 LEAGUES UNDER THE SEA

Words and Music by
Norman Gimbel and Al Hoffman

Melody:

Got   a   whale of a tale to   tell   ya,

D7   G   G7   C   G#°7   Am7

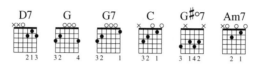

2 1 3   3 2   4   3 2   1   3 2   1   3 1 4 2   2   1

| | |
Chorus 1

        D7 G   G7 C   G
        Got a whale of a tale to tell ya, lads,

              G#°7 Am7
        A whale of a tale or two

        D7   G   G7   C   D7
        'Bout the flappin' fish and the girls I've loved,

        G   D7   G
        On nights like this with the moon above.

             D7   G   C
        A whale of a tale and it's all true,

        G   D7   G
        I swear by my tat - too.

Verse 1

               C   G   G7
        There was Mermaid Minnie,   met her down in Mada - gascar,

        C   G   G7
        She would kiss me   anytime that I would ask her.

        C   G   D7
        Then one evening her flame of love blew out.

        G
        Blow me down and pick me up!

           Am7   D7 G
        She swapped me for a trout.

© 1953 Wonderland Music Company, Inc.
Copyright Renewed
All Rights Reserved   Used by Permission

Chorus 2   *Repeat Chorus 1*

Verse 2

                    C   G   G7
There was Typhoon Tessie,   met her on the coast of Java,

C   G   G7
When we kissed I   bubbled up like molten lava.

C   G   D7
Then she gave me the scare of my young life.

G
Blow me down and pick me up!

        Am7   D7   G
She was the captain's wife.

Chorus 3

D7 G   G7 C   G
Got a whale of a tale to tell ya, lads,

            G#°7 Am7
A whale of a tale or two

D7   G   G7   C   D7
  'Bout the flappin' fish and the girls I've loved,

    G   D7   G
On nights like this with the moon above.

            D7   G   G#°7
A whale of a tale and it's all true,

    Am7   D7   G
I swear by my tat - too.

A Whole New World
from Walt Disney's ALADDIN

Music by Alan Menken
Lyrics by Tim Rice

Melody:

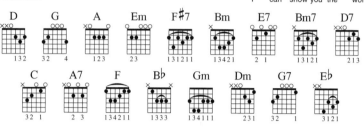

I can show you the world,

D   G   A   Em   F#7   Bm   E7   Bm7   D7

C   A7   F   B♭   Gm   Dm   G7   E♭

Verse 1

　　　　　　　　　　　D
Aladdin: I can show you the world,

　　　　　　　　　　　　　　G   A
Shining, shimmering, splen - did.

Em   F#7　　　Bm　　　　　　　G　　　　　　　D
Tell me princess, now when did you last let your heart de - cide?

Verse 2

　　　　　　　　D
I can open your eyes,

　　　　　　　　　　　　　G   A
Take you wonder by won - der.

Em   F#7　　　　Bm
Over, sideways and under

　　G　　　　　　D
On a magic carpet ride.

Chorus 1

　　　　　　　　　A　　　D　　　　　A　　　　　　　　D
A whole new world,　a new fan - tastic point of view.

　　　　　　　G　　　D   G　　　D
No one to tell us no or where to go

　　Bm　　　　E7　　　　　G
Or say we're only dream - ing.

　　　　　　　　　　　　　　A　　　D　　　　　A　　　　　　Bm7
Jasmine: A whole new world,　a dazzling place I never knew.

D7　　　　　G　　　D　　　　G　　　D
But, when I'm way up here, it's crystal clear

　　Bm7　　E7   C　　　　A7　　　　D
That now I'm in a whole new world with you.

Aladdin: Now I'm in a whole new world with you.

© 1992 Wonderland Music Company, Inc. and Walt Disney Music Company
All Rights Reserved   Used by Permission

Verse 3

               F   Bb C
Jasmine: Unbelievable sights, indescribable feel - ing.

Gm   A7   Dm
Soaring, tumbling, free - wheeling

        Bb   F
Through an endless diamond sky.

             C   F   C   F
A whole new world,   a hundred thousand things to see.

        Bb   F   Bb   F
I'm like a shooting star, I've come so far,

Dm   G7   Bb   C
I can't go back to where I used to be.

Bridge

                   F
Ev'ry turn a sur - prise.

C   Dm
  Ev'ry moment red letter.

F   Bb F
I'll chase them any - where.

    Bb   F
There's time to spare.

Dm G7   Eb   C   Dm
Let me share this whole new world with you.

Outro

          F   Bb   F
Aladdin: A whole new world, *Jasmine:* A whole new world,

                      Gm   F
Aladdin: That's where we'll be. *Jasmine:* That's where we'll be.

               Bb   C
Aladdin: A thrilling chase *Jasmine:* A wond'rous place

           F
Both: For you and me.

Wringle Wrangle
(A Pretty Woman's Love)
from Walt Disney's
WESTWARD HO THE WAGONS

Words and Music by
Stan Jones

Melody:

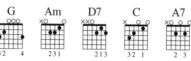

Oh!   Oh!   Wrin - gle, wran - gle,

| G | Am | D7 | C | A7 |

Chorus 1

          G   Am   G   Am
Oh! Oh! Wringle, wrangle, jing-a-jong jangle.

N.C.   G   Am D7 G   Am
 Hey! A mighty fine horse I'm in love of course

        G C   D7   G
 'Cause I got me a pretty woman's love.

Chorus 2

          Am   G   Am
Oh, wringle, wrangle, jing-a-jong jangle.

N.C.   G   Am D7 G   Am
 Hey! A mighty fine horse I'm in love of course

D7   G C   D7   G
 'Cause I got me a pretty woman's love.

Verse

        D7   G   D7   G
With a dollar's worth of beans, a new pair of jeans,

       A7   D7
Got a woman to cook and wash and things.

Outro-Chorus

       G   Am   G   Am
Wringle, wrangle, jing-a-jong jangle.

N.C.   G Am D7 G   Am
 Hey! And if I die   I   ain't a gonna cry

D7   G C   D7   G
 'Cause I got me a pretty woman's love.

D7   G C   D7   G
Yes, I got me a pretty woman's love.

              C   D7 G N.C.
Yes, I got me a pretty wom - an's love. Hey!

© 1956 Walt Disney Music Company
Copyright Renewed
All Rights Reserved Used by Permission

Written in the Stars

from Elton John and Tim Rice's AIDA

Music by Elton John
Lyrics by Tim Rice

Melody:

I am here to tell — you

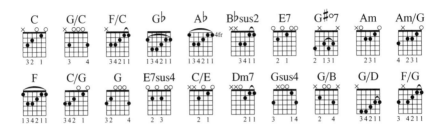

Intro | C G/C F/C | C G/C F/C | G♭ A♭ B♭sus2 |

Verse 1
                C   G/C F/C   C   E7 G#°7
Male: I am here to tell   you we can never meet again.

  Am   Am/G
Simple really, isn't it?

   F   C/G G C   G/C F/C
A word or two and then   a lifetime of not know-ing

          C   E7sus4 E7
Where or how or why or when

        Am   Am/G   F   C/E
You think of me or speak of me or wonder what befell

      Dm7   C/G   G
The someone you once loved so long a-go, so well.

© 1999 Wonderland Music Company, Inc., Happenstance Ltd. and Evadon Ltd.
All Rights Reserved   Used by Permission

Verse 2

           C   G/C F/C   C   E7sus4 E7
Female: Never wonder what   I'll feel as living shuffles by.

Am   Am/G   F   Gsus4 G/B
You don't have to ask me and I need not reply.

C   G/D F/C   C   E7sus4 E7
Ev'ry moment of   my life from now until I die

Am   Am/G   F   C/E
I will think or dream of you and fail to understand

          Dm7   C/G   G
How a perfect love can be confounded out of hand.

Chorus 1

           C   G/B
Both: Is it written in the stars?

          Am   C/G
Are we paying for some crime?

          F   Dm7   C/G
Is that all that we are good for, just a stretch of mortal time?

G   C   G/B Am   Am/G
Is this God's experiment   in which we have no say?

     F
In which we're given paradise,

      Dm7 C/G G   C   G/C F/C   C   G/C F/C
But only   for   a day?

Verse 3

           C   G/C F/C
Male: Nothing can be al - tered.

             C   E7sus4 E7
Oh, there is nothing to decide.

Am   Am/G   F   Gsus4 G/B
No escape, no change of heart, nor any place to hide.

           C   G/D F/C   C   E7sus4 E7
Female: You're all I ev - er want but this I am denied.

Am   Am/G   F   C/E
Sometimes in my darkest thoughts I wish I never learned

          Dm7   C/G   G
Both: What it is to be in love and have that love returned.

	C
Chorus 2	*Both:* Is it written in the stars?

G/B   Am   Am/G
Oh, are we paying for some crime?

    F   C/E   Dm7   C/G
Is that all that we are good for,   just a stretch of mortal time?

G   C   G/B   Am   Am/G
Is this God's experiment, oh, in which we have no say?

   F   Dm7 F/G   C
In which we're given paradise, but only   for a day?

              G/B
(Is it written in the stars?)

    Am   Am/G
(Are we paying for some crime?)

   F   Dm7   F/G
(Is that all that we are good for, just a stretch of mortal time?)

          C   G/B   Am
Both: Is this God's experiment *Male:*   in   which we have no say?

              Am/G
Female: In which we have ____ no say,

     F
Male: In which we're given paradise *Female:* Given paradise

    Dm7   F/G   C
Both: Only   for a day.

| *Outro* | ǀ C   G/C F/C ǀ C   G/C F/C ǀ G♭ A♭ B♭sus2 ǀ C |

Yo Ho

(A Pirate's Life for Me)
from PIRATES OF THE CARIBBEAN
at Disneyland Park and
Magic Kingdom Park

Words by Xavier Atencio
Music by George Bruns

Melody:

Yo ho,   yo ho,   a

G   C   D7   Em   B7   Am   A7

Verse 1

> G   C G   D7   G
> Yo ho, yo ho, a pirate's life for me.
>
>   Em   B7
> We pillage, plunder, we rifle and loot.
>
>   Em   B7
> Drink up me 'earties, yo ho.
>
>   Am   D7   G   Em
> We kidnap and ravage and don't give a hoot.
>
>   A7   D7
> Drink up me 'earties, yo ho.

Verse 2

> G   C G   D7   G
> Yo ho, yo ho, a pirate's life for me.
>
>   Em   B7
> We extort and pilfer, we filch and sack.
>
>   Em   B7
> Drink up me 'earties, yo ho.
>
>   Am   D7   G   Em
> Ma - raud and em - bezzle and even hi - jack.
>
>   A7   D7
> Drink up me 'earties, yo ho.

© 1967 Walt Disney Music Company
Copyright Renewed
All Rights Reserved   Used by Permission

Verse 3

```
         G   C G        D7    G
Yo ho, yo ho, a pirate's life for me.

    Em                  B7
We kindle and char and in - flame and ignite.

    Em                  B7
Drink up me 'earties, yo ho.

    Am       D7      G     Em
We burn up the city, we're really a fright.

    A7               D7
Drink up me 'earties, yo ho.
```

Outro

```
B7     Em                      B7
  We're rascals and scoundrels, we're villains and knaves.

    Em           B7
Drink up me 'earties, yo ho.

    Am       D7            G     Em
We're devils and black sheep, we're really bad eggs.

    A7               D7
Drink up me 'earties, yo ho.

G    C  G        D7    G
Yo ho, yo  ho, a pirate's life for me.
```

You'll Be in My Heart (Pop Version)

from Walt Disney Pictures' TARZAN TM

Words and Music by
Phil Collins

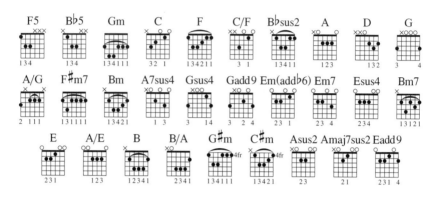

Intro

F5
Come stop your crying, it will be all right.

Just take my hand, hold it tight.

B♭5
I will protect you from all around you.

Gm   **C**
I will be here, don't you ___ cry.

Verse 1

F   **C/F**   **F**
For one so small you seem so strong.

                           C/F   **F**
My arms will hold you, keep you safe and warm.

B♭sus2
This bond between us can't be broken.

Gm   **C**
I will be here, don't you ___ cry.

© 1999 Edgar Rice Burroughs, Inc. and Walt Disney Music Company
All Rights Reserved   Used by Permission

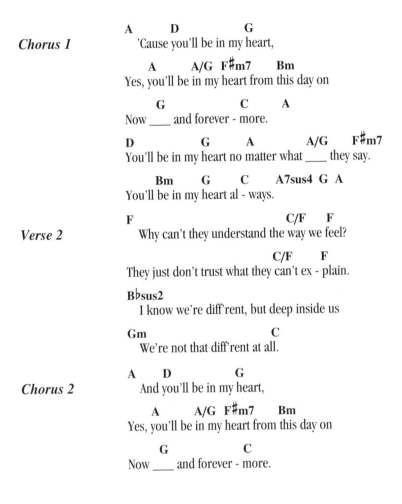

Chorus 1

A   D   G
'Cause you'll be in my heart,

A   A/G F#m7   Bm
Yes, you'll be in my heart from this day on

G   C   A
Now ___ and forever - more.

D   G   A   A/G   F#m7
You'll be in my heart no matter what ___ they say.

Bm   G   C   A7sus4 G A
You'll be in my heart al - ways.

Verse 2

F   C/F   F
Why can't they understand the way we feel?

                             C/F   F
They just don't trust what they can't ex - plain.

B♭sus2
I know we're diff'rent, but deep inside us

Gm   C
We're not that diff'rent at all.

Chorus 2

A   D   G
And you'll be in my heart,

A   A/G F#m7   Bm
Yes, you'll be in my heart from this day on

G   C
Now ___ and forever - more.

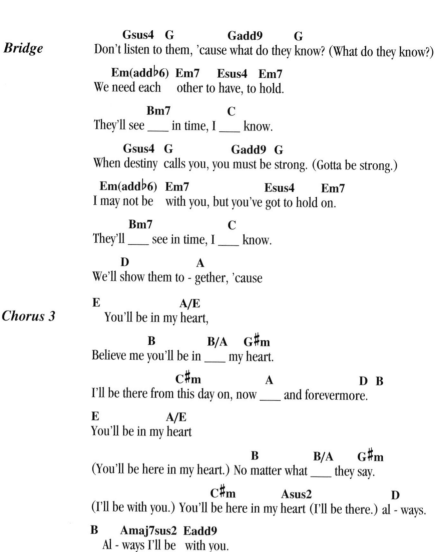

Bridge

Gsus4 G   Gadd9   G
Don't listen to them, 'cause what do they know? (What do they know?)

Em(add♭6) Em7   Esus4 Em7
We need each   other to have, to hold.

    Bm7   C
They'll see ___ in time, I ___ know.

    Gsus4 G   Gadd9 G
When destiny calls you, you must be strong. (Gotta be strong.)

 Em(add♭6) Em7   Esus4   Em7
I may not be   with you, but you've got to hold on.

    Bm7   C
They'll ___ see in time, I ___ know.

    D   A
We'll show them to - gether, 'cause

Chorus 3

E   A/E
  You'll be in my heart,

        B   B/A   G♯m
Believe me you'll be in ___ my heart.

        C♯m   A   D B
I'll be there from this day on, now ___ and forevermore.

E   A/E
You'll be in my heart

                B   B/A   G♯m
(You'll be here in my heart.) No matter what ___ they say.

        C♯m   Asus2   D
(I'll be with you.) You'll be here in my heart (I'll be there.) al - ways.

B   Amaj7sus2 Eadd9
 Al - ways I'll be   with you.

   Amaj7sus2   Eadd9
I'll be there for you always, always and al - ways.

   Amaj7sus2   Eadd9
Just look o - ver your shoulder. Just look o - ver your shoulder.

   Amaj7sus2   E Eadd9
Just look o - ver your shoulder, I'll be there always.

Zip-A-Dee-Doo-Dah
from Walt Disney's SONG OF THE SOUTH

Words by Ray Gilbert
Music by Allie Wrubel

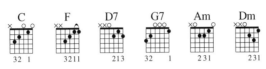

Verse 1

    C   F   C
Zip-a-dee-doo-dah, zip-a-dee-ay,

F   C   D7   G7
My, oh my, what a wonderful day!

C   F   C
Plenty of sunshine, headin' my way.

F   C   Am Dm G7 C
Zip-a-dee-doo - dah,   zip-a-dee-ay!

Bridge

      G7   C
Mister Bluebird on my shoulder.

      D7
It's the truth, it's "actch'll."

G N.C.
Ev'rything is "satisfactch'll."

Verse 2

    C   F   C
Zip-a-dee-doo-dah, zip-a-dee-ay!

F   C Am D7   G7 C
Wonderful feel - ing, wonder-ful day.

© 1945 Walt Disney Music Company
Copyright Renewed
All Rights Reserved   Used by Permission

Guitar Chord Songbooks

Each book includes complete lyrics, chord symbols, and guitar chord diagrams.

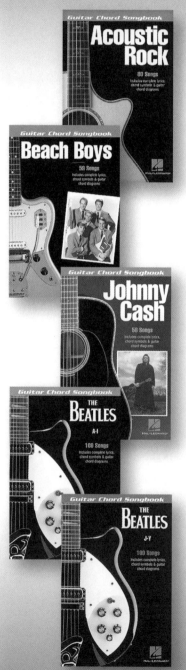

Acoustic Rock
80 acoustic favorites: Blackbird • Blowin' in the Wind • Layla • Maggie May • Me and Julio down by the Schoolyard • Pink Houses • and more.
00699540...$17.95

Alabama
50 of Alabama's best: Born Country • Dixieland Delight • Feels So Right • Mountain Music • Song of the South • Why Lady Why • and more.
00699914 ....$14.95

The Beach Boys
59 favorites: California Girls • Don't Worry Baby • Fun, Fun, Fun • Good Vibrations • Help Me Rhonda • Wouldn't It Be Nice • dozens more!
00699566...$14.95

Blues
80 blues tunes: Big Boss Man • Cross Road Blues (Crossroads) • Damn Right, I've Got the Blues • Pride and Joy • Route 66 • Sweet Home Chicago • and more.
00699733 ....$12.95

Broadway
80 stage hits: All I Ask of You • Bali Ha'i • Edelweiss • Hello, Dolly! • Memory • Ol' Man River • People • Seasons of Love • Sunrise, Sunset • and more.
00699920 ....$14.99

Johnny Cash
58 Cash classics: A Boy Named Sue • Cry, Cry, Cry • Daddy Sang Bass • Folsom Prison Blues • I Walk the Line • RIng of Fire • Solitary Man • and more.
00699648...$16.95

The Beatles (A-I)
An awesome reference of Beatles hits: All You Need Is Love • The Ballad of John and Yoko • Get Back • Good Day Sunshine • A Hard Day's Night • Hey Jude • I Saw Her Standing There • and more!
00699558...$17.99

The Beatles (J-Y)
100 more Beatles hits: Lady Madonna • Let It Be • Ob-La-Di, Ob-La-Da • Paperback Writer • Revolution • Twist and Shout • When I'm Sixty-Four • and more.
00699562...$17.99

Steven Curtis Chapman
65 from this CCM superstar: Be Still and Know • Cinderella • For the Sake of the Call • Live Out Loud • Speechless • With Hope • and more.
00700702 ....$14.99

Children's Songs
70 songs for kids: Alphabet Song • Bingo • The Candy Man • Eensy Weensy Spider • Puff the Magic Dragon • Twinkle, Twinkle Little Star • and more!
00699539...$14.95

Complete contents listings available online at www.halleonard.com

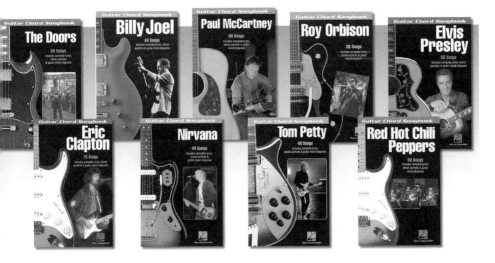

Christmas Carols
80 Christmas carols: Angels We Have Heard on High • The Holly and the Ivy • I Saw Three Ships • Joy to the World • O Holy Night • Silent Night • What Child Is This? • and more.
00699536..$12.95

Christmas Songs
80 Christmas favorites: The Christmas Song • Feliz Navidad • Jingle-Bell Rock • Merry Christmas, Darling • Rudolph the Red-Nosed Reindeer • more.
00699537..$12.95

Eric Clapton
75 of Slowhand's finest: I Shot the Sheriff • Knockin' on Heaven's Door • Layla • Strange Brew • Tears in Heaven • Wonderful Tonight • and more!
00699567..$15.99

Classic Rock
80 rock essentials: Beast of Burden • Cat Scratch Fever • Hot Blooded • Money • Rhiannon • Sweet Emotion • Walk on the Wild Side • more
00699598..$15.99

Contemporary Christian
80 hits from today's top CCM artists: Awesome God • El Shaddai • Friends • His Strength Is Perfect • I Will Be Here • A Maze of Grace • Run to You • more.
00699564..$14.95

Country
80 country standards: Boot Scootin' Boogie • Crazy • Hey, Good Lookin' • Sixteen Tons • Through the Years • Your Cheatin' Heart • more.
00699534..$14.95

Country Favorites
Over 60 songs: Achy Breaky Heart (Don't Tell My Heart) • Brand New Man • Gone Country • The Long Black Veil • Make the World Go Away • and more.
00700609 ....$14.99

Country Standards
60 songs: By the Time I Get to Phoenix • El Paso • The Gambler • I Fall to Pieces • Jolene • King of the Road • Put Your Hand in the Hand • A Rainy Night in Georgia • more.
00700608 ....$12.95

Cowboy Songs
Over 60 tunes: Back in the Saddle Again • Happy Trails • Home on the Range • Streets of Laredo • The Yellow Rose of Texas • and more.
00699636..$12.95

The Doors
60 classics: Break on Through to the Other Side • The End • L.A. Woman • Light My Fire • Love Her Madly • Love Me Two Times • People Are Strange • Riders on the Storm • Twentieth Century Fox • and more.
00699888 ....$15.99

Early Rock
80 early rock classics: All I Have to Do Is Dream • Fever • He's So Fine • I'm Sorry • Lollipop • Puppy Love • Sh-Boom (Life Could Be a Dream) • and more.
00699916 ....$14.99

Folk Pop Rock
80 songs: American Pie • Dust in the Wind • Me and Bobby McGee • Somebody to Love • Time in a Bottle • and more.
00699651..$14.95

Folksongs
80 folk favorites: Aura Lee • Camptown Races • Danny Boy • Man of Constant Sorrow • Nobody Knows the Trouble I've Seen • When the Saints Go Marching In • and more.
00699541..$12.95

Gospel Hymns
80 hymns: Amazing Grace • Give Me That Old Time Religion • I Love to Tell the Story • The Old Rugged Cross • Shall We Gather at the River? • Wondrous Love • and more.
00700463 ....$14.99

Grand Ole Opry®
80 great songs: Abilene • Act Naturally • Country Boy • Crazy • Friends in Low Places • He Stopped Loving Her Today • Wings of.a Dove • dozens more!
00699885 ....$16.95

Hillsong United
65 top worship songs: Break Free • Everyday • From the Inside Out • God Is Great • Look to You • Now That You're Near • Salvation Is Here • To the Ends of the Earth • and more.
00700222 ....$12.95

Jazz Standards
50 songs: Ain't Misbehavin' • Cheek to Cheek • In the Wee Small Hours of the Morning • The Nearness of You • Stardust • The Way You Look Tonight • and more.
00700972 ....$14.95

Billy Joel
60 Billy Joel favorites: It's Still Rock and Roll to Me • The Longest Time • Piano Man • She's Always a Woman • Uptown Girl • We Didn't Start the Fire • You May Be Right • and more.
00699632...$15.99

Elton John
60 songs: Bennie and the Jets • Candle in the Wind • Crocodile Rock • Goodbye Yellow Brick Road • Pinball Wizard • Sad Songs (Say So Much) • Tiny Dancer • Your Song • and more.
00699732 ....$15.99

Latin
60 favorites: Bésame Mucho (Kiss Me Much) • The Girl from Ipanema (Garôta De Ipanema) • The Look of Love • So Nice (Summer Samba) • and more.
00700973 ....$14.95

Paul McCartney
60 from Sir Paul: Band on the Run • Jet • Let 'Em In • Maybe I'm Amazed • No More Lonely Nights • Say Say Say • Take It Away • With a Little Luck • more!
00385035 ....$16.95

Motown
60 Motown masterpieces: ABC • Baby I Need Your Lovin' • I'll Be There • Just My Imagination • Lady Marmalade • Stop! In the Name of Love • You Can't Hurry Love • more.
00699734 ....$16.95

The 1950s
80 early rock favorites: High Hopes • Mister Sandman • Only You (And You Alone) • Put Your Head on My Shoulder • Que Sera, Sera (Whatever Will Be, Will Be) • Tammy • That's Amoré • and more.
00699922 ....$14.99

The 1980s
80 hits: Centerfold • Come on Eileen • Don't Worry, Be Happy • Got My Mind Set on You • Sailing • Should I Stay or Should I Go • Sweet Dreams (Are Made of This) • more.
00700551 ....$16.99

Nirvana
40 songs: About a Girl • Come as You Are • Heart Shaped Box • The Man Who Sold the World • Smells like Teen Spirit • You Know You're Right • and more.
00699762 ....$16.99

Roy Orbison
38 songs: Blue Bayou • Crying • Oh, Pretty Woman • Only the Lonely (Know the Way I Feel) • Pretty Paper • Running Scared • Working for the Man • You Got It • and more.
00699752 ....$12.95

Tom Petty
American Girl • Breakdown • Don't Do Me like That • Free Fallin' • Here Comes My Girl • Into the Great Wide Open • Mary Jane's Last Dance • Refugee • Runnin' Down a Dream • The Waiting • more.
00699883 ....$15.99

Pop/Rock
80 chart hits: Against All Odds • Come Sail Away • Every Breath You Take • Hurts So Good • Kokomo • More Than Words • Smooth • Summer of '69 • and more.
00699538...$14.95

Praise and Worship
80 favorites: Agnus Dei • He Is Exalted • I Could Sing of Your Love Forever • Lord, I Lift Your Name on High • More Precious Than Silver • Open the Eyes of My Heart • Shine, Jesus, Shine • and more.
00699634 ....$12.95

Elvis Presley
60 hits: All Shook Up • Blue Suede Shoes • Can't Help Falling in Love • Heartbreak Hotel • Hound Dog • Jailhouse Rock • Suspicious Minds • Viva Las Vegas • more.
00699633...$14.95

Red Hot Chili Peppers
50 hits: Breaking the Girl • By the Way • Californication • Give It Away • Higher Ground • Love Rollercoaster • Scar Tissue • Suck My Kiss • Under the Bridge • What It Is • and more.
00699710...$16.95

Rock 'n' Roll
80 rock 'n' roll classics: At the Hop • Great Balls of Fire • It's My Party • La Bamba • My Boyfriend's Back • Peggy Sue • Stand by Me • more.
00699535...$14.95

Sting
50 favorites from Sting and the Police: Brand New Day • Can't Stand Losing You • Don't Stand So Close to Me • Every Breath You Take • Fields of Gold • King of Pain • Message in a Bottle • Roxanne • more.
00699921 ....$14.99

Three Chord Songs
65 includes: All Right Now • La Bamba • Lay Down Sally • Mony, Mony • Rock Around the Clock • Rock This Town • Werewolves of London • You Are My Sunshine • and more.
00699720 ....$12.95

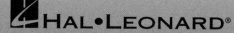

HAL•LEONARD®

Prices, contents and availability subject to change without notice.

0709